D0941419

Every system of religious belief has attempted an explanation of undeserved suffering. Father Sutcliffe first discusses the solutions offered by some of the great religious systems of the past. He then goes on to the Hebrew attitude as revealed in the Old Testament—the question of sin and its consequences, the ideas of corporate solidarity and individual responsibility, vicarious suffering, the bewilderment of the Psalmist and of Job and their faith in God through it all. Then follows the idea of suffering in the light of the future life, the teaching of the New Testament and the divine precepts and example of Christ.

Providence and Suffering

in the

Old and New Testaments

By the same author

A Two-Year Ministry (Burns & Oates)

The Old Testament and the Future Life (Burns & Oates)

A Grammar of the Maltese Language (Oxford University Press)

Providence and Suffering in the Old and New Testaments

by

EDMUND F. SUTCLIFFE S.J.

Professor of Old Testament Exegesis and Hebrew at Heythrop College

THOMAS NELSON AND SONS LTD

London Edinburgh Paris Melbourne Toronto and New York

De Licentia Superiorum Ordinis :

D. BOYLE S.J.
Praep. Prov. Angliae

Nihil obstat :

RICARDUS J. FOSTER S.T.L. L.S.S.
Censor Deputatus

Imprimatur :

✠ HUMPHREIUS BRIGHT
Episcopus Tit. Solensis
Vicarius Generalis Birmingamiensis

Die 13 Nov. 1953

THOMAS NELSON AND SONS LTD
Parkside Works Edinburgh 9
36 Park Street London W1
312 Flinders Street Melbourne C1
218 Grand Parade Centre Cape Town

THOMAS NELSON AND SONS (CANADA) LTD
91–93 Wellington Street West Toronto 1

THOMAS NELSON AND SONS
19 East 47th Street New York 17

SOCIÉTÉ FRANÇAISE D'EDITIONS NELSON
25 rue Henri Barbusse Paris V^{e}

CONTENTS

ABBREVIATIONS

BZAW Beiheft der Zeitschrift für die Alttestamentliche Wissenschaft

CC *A Catholic Commentary on Holy Scripture* (London 1953)

Conteneau, *L'Épopée*
G. Conteneau, *L'Épopée de Gilgamesh* (Paris 1939)

CSEL Corpus Scriptorum Ecclesiasticorum Latinorum

DAFC *Dictionnaire apologétique de la Foi catholique*

Dhorme, *Choix*
P. Dhorme, *Choix de textes religieux assyro-babyloniens* (Études bibliques ; Paris 1907)

DV Douay Version

ERE Hastings' *Encyclopaedia of Religion and Ethics*

ET *Expository Times*

Gelin, *Idées*
A. Gelin P.S.S., *Les idées maîtresses de l'Ancien Testament* (Paris 1948 ; Lectio Divina 2)

Gressmann, *Texte*
H. Gressmann, *Altorientalische Texte zum alten Testament* (Berlin und Leipzig 1926^{2})

HT Hebrew text

Huby, *Christus*
J. Huby, edit., *Christus : Manuel d'histoire de religions* (Paris 1912^{6})

Jastrow, *Religion*
M. Jastrow Jr., *The Religion of Babylonia and Assyria* (Boston, etc. 1898)

JNES *Journal of Near Eastern Studies*

JTS *Journal of Theological Studies*

Lectures (CTS)
Lectures on the History of Religions (Catholic Truth Society)

LXX Septuagint

Migne, PG Migne, *Patrologia Graeca*

Migne, PL Migne, *Patrologia Latina* (first edition)

Peake, *Problem*
A. S. Peake, *The Problem of Suffering in the Old Testament* (London 1904 ; 1947)

Abbreviations

Pritchard, *Texts*

J. B. Pritchard, edit., *Ancient Near Eastern Texts relating to the Old Testament* (Princeton 1950)

RB *Revue Biblique*

RV Revised Version

Rowley, *Submission*

H. H. Rowley, *Submission in Suffering and other Essays on Eastern Thought* (Cardiff 1951)

Stamm, *Leiden*

J. J. Stamm, *Das Leiden des Unschuldigen in Babylon und Israel* (Zurich 1946)

Sutcliffe, *Future Life*

E. F. Sutcliffe S.J., *The Old Testament and the Future Life* (The Bellarmine Series ; London 1947[2])

Thompson, *Epic*

R. Campbell Thompson, *The Epic of Gilgamish* (London 1928)

VD *Verbum Domini*

VDBS Vigouroux, *Dictionnaire de la Bible, Supplément*

VT *Vetus Testamentum*

WV Westminster Version

OTHER BOOKS

M. D'Arcy S.J.: *The Pain of this World and the Providence of God* (London, new ed. 1953)

E. G. King : *Early Religious Poetry of the Hebrews* (Cambridge 1911), chap. 5 ' The Problem of Suffering '

H. Schmidt : *Gott und das Leid im Alten Testament* (Giessen 1926)

A. B. Davidson : *The Theology of the Old Testament* (Edinburgh 1904)

P. Heinisch : *Theologie des Alten Testamentes* (Bonn 1940 ; Bonner Bibel, Ergänzungsband I)

W. Eichrodt : *Theologie des Alten Testaments* (Berlin 1950) I[4], II[3], III[3]

G. Procksch : *Theologie des Alten Testaments* (Gütersloh 1950)

Chapter I

SOME ANCIENT VIEWS

Greek, Roman, Egyptian

The existence of suffering in this world is a fact which requires no demonstration. It is within the experience of us all, even of the young. We do not need to seek for it; it thrusts itself on our notice. Such too is its universality that the Church in an oft repeated prayer calls this world of ours a 'vale of tears'. And a Roman philosopher who did not deny the existence of the gods, none the less persuaded himself that man's habitation could not have been prepared for him by divine power, being characterised, as it is, by elements of harm and disorder. For thus Lucretius undertook to prove

> nequaquam nobis divinitus esse paratam
> naturam rerum; tanta stat prædita culpa

and he goes on to say that it is only fitting that the new-born infant should celebrate its arrival on earth by wailing seeing that it shall have in life such an experience of evils:

> vagituque locum lugubri complet, ut aecumst
> cui tantum in vita restet transire malorum.[1]

As man has a natural craving for happiness implanted in his being by the Creator, this universal presence of suffering in our midst calls for an explanation in every system of religious belief. A special aspect of the question is that concerning the suffering of the innocent. On this Moses Gaster, the late Chief Rabbi of the Spanish and Portuguese Congregations, London, wrote that 'the grave problem which has haunted every form of faith has been: how to reconcile the happiness

[1] *De Rerum Natura* V 198f., 226f.

of the sinner and the trials and sufferings of the pious and good with the justice of God '.[1] However, as will appear, in some religious systems the suffering of the innocent presents no problem at all for the simple reason that according to their tenets the innocent do not suffer, or, in other words, as no one is innocent, the supposed problem is built on a false presupposition and is therefore fictitious.

Our own special field of inquiry is that presented by the books of the Old Testament, but before we enter that field it will be well to call to mind the solutions of the problem of suffering proposed by some of the great religious systems of the past, especially those of the ancient East. With the outline of these beliefs in mind we shall be in a better position to form a fair estimate of the truth and value of the conceptions entertained by the ancient Hebrews. And as background to all these views we have the Christian belief which I propose in the words of E. Lemme : ' It is one of the noblest paradoxes of Christianity that sufferings according to the Christian outlook on life have intrinsic value. According to the ordinary view that is an evil which impairs the impulse to self-preservation, and that is a good thing which favours it. According to the Christian view of the Kingdom of God as the highest good an evil in Christian thought is that which hinders self-preservation for eternal life (Mk 8:36), and a good thing in Christian thought is whatever promotes self-preservation for eternal life (Lk 10:42). Thus the Christian conception is in various respects precisely the opposite of the natural. . . . In the matter of suffering this distinction is fundamental in that the world experiences suffering as an evil whereas Christianity reckons it among the conditions ordained and willed by God for the attainment of our eternal destiny (Rom 8:17f., 2 Cor 4:15) '.[2]

In India the belief that has survived for millennia in Brahmanism or Hinduism is that the suffering undergone by every human being is the aftermath of wrongdoing com-

[1] ERE XII 437*b*

[2] *Realencyklopädie für protestantische Theologie und Kirche.* J. J. Herzog-A. Hauck. XI (Leipzig 1902³) 360

mitted during a previous state of existence. This is the law of *karma*. Suffering is therefore merited retribution. The theory provides an explanation applicable to all human beings, whether infant or adult, for although the infant is incapable of doing evil in its present incarnation, it will have been guilty in some way in a previous existence. It also provides an answer to the problem of the suffering endured by animals, for in the process of *samsāra* or transmigration of souls into new bodies after death the new habitation may be not that of a human being but that of some member of the brute creation. This doctrine is linked up with a pessimistic view of life. As we experience it, life is separated off or broken up into innumerable individual existences and this is necessarily bad, as it involves separation from the universal soul. That is where men really belong and there can be no true happiness as long as this separation continues. Hence the purpose of men must be to bring the process of *samsāra* to an end when the soul loses its individual existence and becomes merged in the world soul. This consummation is brought about when the 'thirst' for existence is extinguished, for this is the ultimate source of all evil. From this doctrine there follows as a corollary the necessity of self-discipline and renunciation. This method of discipline is called *Yoga*, which in its complete course comprises both psychical and physical exercises. It should be added that even after the complete extinction of the evil 'thirst', individual existence may yet continue for some time as the power of *karma* may not by that time have been completely extinguished.

This doctrine is not without its weak points. Men, normally at least, have no recollection whatever of any previous existence nor of any acts, whether good or bad, for which they were responsible before their present incarnation. Consequently, though they must acknowledge their guilt and the justice of the retribution which is their lot, they are in complete ignorance of how the guilt was incurred and there is no possibility of repentance for their specific acts of wrongdoing. Moreover, the doctrine does not explain the measure of suffering that befalls a human being in his first incarnation, for according to the *Mahābhārata* 'the measure of weal or woe is dependent on the acts of a previous life'.[1] The chain is thus left without a first link and is presented, as it were, hanging in the air. The system also leads to the very unfortunate result that it tends to crush the feeling of pity and commiseration in the heart. And the reason, which springs from the system itself, is that its adherents must regard every sufferer as guilty and receiving the due punishment of his guilt. It is only fair to add that, on the contrary, the system has been presented as one of universal love. Thus Mahendranath Sircar writes: 'Carrying the most kindly feeling for all, regarding every self as his own self, unconcerned with the sweetness or bitterness of life, the wanderer moves as the figure of wisdom and love harmoniously set to each other—wisdom saves his self, love saves others'.[2] The ground of this view of every self being one's own self is the identity of each and every self with the Cosmic Being: 'The Upanisadic Mysticism does not leave the least distinction between the Cosmic Being without and the vivifying Self within'.[3] But how many, it may be asked, share the knowledge of this identity, which is the basis necessary to support this universal charity? Sircar himself supplies the answer earlier in his book where he uses the word 'God', evidently a pantheistic God, to signify the Cosmic Being: 'The Upanisads do not recognise the least difference between man and God, but this wisdom is vouchsafed only to the few'.[4] This evidently means that for the vast majority this source of kindly feeling is closed and sealed. That Indian renunciation and asceticism is in the main wholly self-regarding and without the spirit of commiseration is illustrated by a remark quoted in the *Church Times*[5]: 'We! We are holy men (Sannyasi); we never do anything for anyone else'. And so, consistently, on the occasion in question, these holy men refused to help to carry a poor sufferer to hospital.

In some of its main features this Brahmanic doctrine is

[1] Quoted by Rowley, *Submission* p. 16
[2] *Hindu Mysticism according to the Upanisads* (London 1934) 308
[3] *Ibid.*, p. 105 [4] *Ibid.*, p. 5
[5] 21 Oct. 1932, p. 490

shared by Buddhism, which arose on Indian soil in the sixth pre-Christian century and afterwards spread to many lands. Its adherents inherited from the older religion the doctrines of *samsāra* and *karma* with their explanation of the world-wide prevalence of suffering. But to the difficulties of the previous system Buddhism adds an even greater. The belief of the older religion is that each man has an individual soul, albeit detached from the World Soul to which it properly belongs and separated from which it is doomed for ever to be a stranger to true happiness. This individual soul is capable of existence after its separation from the body at death and passes at once into a new body and so into a fresh earthly existence corresponding to the measure of its merits and demerits in its preceding incarnation. It is the same soul and so can carry its burden of guilt with it, although in its new body it has no recollection of its previous actions or of what constituted its guilt. But according to Buddhist doctrine men have no souls. There is no such thing as an 'Ego', no such thing as a person remaining ever identical with himself through all the flux of change. Man is only a concatenation of thoughts, feelings, perceptions, and the like. There is no being within that thinks, feels, or perceives. Man may be compared to a manufactured article such as a carriage. When we see the different parts conjoined, the wheels, the axle, the body and the rest, we call it a carriage. Still we know that it is only a combination of parts, which are in reality separate, independent beings without any intrinsic unity. So it is with man. The human being is merely a bundle of co-existing elements devoid of any intrinsic unity, without a soul to which these various elements can belong. None the less we are right in regarding each such bundle of phenomena as a unit and denoting it by a separate name. The flame which is burning on a candle now is not the flame that was burning on it a short while ago. Yet there is an unbroken continuity and it remains the same flame. Similarly, the water that flows by at my feet in a river is not the water that flowed by some minutes before, and in course of time none of the water within the banks of the river is the same water that was there before. Yet it remains ever the same river and is rightly designated by the same name. So it is with man. His life is a Heraclitean flux, ever changing, never the same for two consecutive moments; yet like the flame and the river it has continuity and at least apparent unity.

But what, it may be asked, is the validity of this doctrine as an explanation of suffering? The difficulty that besets the older doctrine is no stranger to this, for again there is no solution of the problem of man's complete ignorance of previous existence and activities and of guilt previously incurred and no explanation of the justice of a system according to which a man is punished for guilt entirely beyond his knowledge. But this difficulty is of small moment compared to the fundamental mystery of how there can be guilt without any person in existence who can be guilty. And even if it be conceded that guilt can attach to a bundle of thoughts, sensations, perceptions and the like, the further problem remains, how such guilt can be transmitted to a future bundle of different thoughts, sensations, and perceptions. The water in the river today cannot be blamed for the devastation wrought by the waters of the river overflowing its banks a month ago.

Another form of this theory of metempsychosis is found among the Kabbalist Jews and, although its appearance is so much later, is worthy of notice here since our main theme concerns the beliefs of Israel. The earliest records of the doctrine date from the ninth or tenth century in such works as the *Zôhār*, but it is always introduced as already familiar to the public for whom the literature is intended, and is nowhere given a systematic exposition. The inference therefore seems justified that the doctrine itself is much older than its first appearance in literature. It has no roots in the Old Testament, though its adherents gave an arbitrary twist to various texts in order to find biblical authority in its support. Some other religion must have been the source of the borrowing which was then fitted into the general scheme of Judaism. Now according to the cosmogony of Genesis God completed the work of creation on the sixth day and then rested from His work on the seventh. Hence, it was deduced, all human souls were created on that day ready in due time to take their places in human bodies. In the meantime their place of abode is in the heavenly courts without distinction of those whose earthly course has already been completed and those yet to come down to earth. When a child is conceived, God designates a soul to be joined in union with it, and despite the soul's unwillingness to leave its celestial abode it must perforce obey. It is forearmed with a knowledge of the other-worldly rewards of virtue and punishments of evil. It thus descends to earth entirely innocent; and, although it retains no clear memory of the warning knowledge received, this is the unconscious basis of its power to distinguish good and evil. The contamination of the material world and the assaults of evil spirits in time succeed in sullying its purity and, it may be, in leading it into iniquity worthy of the punishment of Gehinnom. In this case, unable to return to Heaven on its separation from the body at death and desirous of avoiding the retribution of Gehinnom, the soul waits its opportunity to enter into a new body so to have the possibility of making atonement for past misdeeds. This furthers the universal good, as the Messianic era cannot begin till all souls have served the purpose of their creation by being united to human bodies and atonement has been made for all evil committed.

This doctrine, it will be seen, provides a solution of the problem why the just should suffer. If a just man is seen in affliction it is because of guilt contracted in a former existence. And if, on the other hand, a wicked man enjoys prosperity and bliss, the explanation is that he is enjoying the reward of good previously done, whereas his punishment for his wickedness is still in store for him.

An entirely different solution of the existence of evil and suffering in the world is that proposed by the Iranian religion of Mazdaeism and Zoroastrianism. According to the adherents of this dualistic system there are two powers from eternity, the power of good and the power of evil. These are Ahura Mazda and Angra Mainyu, the Good Spirit and the Destroying

Spirit, who are known in later Persian literature under the names of Ormazd and Ahriman. Between these two there is a perpetual conflict. Both are creators, and all that is evil and noxious in the world is the work of the evil creator. To him belong the lesser evil spirits and all that is physically harmful such as diseases, poisonous plants, and noxious animals. The system is dualistic, as both powers exist in entire independence of each other, both have their being from eternity, and both are creators in their own right. Still, good is to triumph finally, and at the end of the world Ahriman and all that is his will be not only finally overcome but will be completely destroyed. Thus, strangely and inconsistently, a monotheistic element enters into this otherwise dualistic system.

The religion of the Egyptians is one of the most interesting and also one of the most baffling. It is impossible to give a short and simple account of the beliefs it enshrines. And this is so, not only because in the course of more than three millennia it underwent development and received accretions, but also because the records even of one and the same period contain so many statements, so many points of view that appear to us mutually exclusive. And this holds good even of the restricted subject that occupies our interest here. At least this may be said without qualification, that suffering does not seem to have been an oppressive problem to the Egyptians. And the explanation appears to be that they believed firmly in the constant and unchangeable order of the world. History and experience alike bear witness that some men are fortunate, others are unfortunate; some enjoy health and strength, others do not. And as nothing can interfere with the order of the universe, established from the time of creation, the Egyptian accepted with patience the lot he conceived to be inevitable. Hence, perhaps, references to suffering in the literature are not common except in texts dealing with life after death, and in these, as will appear below, the sting of the thought is removed by the complete confidence that it will not be experienced.

There are passages which imply punishment for evil done. So in a prayer to Re (Ra): 'Punish me not for my many sins '.[1] In the Teaching of Ptahhotep, according to the interpretation of Wallis Budge, the father of a son who does evilly should cast him out and God will punish him.[2] But in Erman's version the sentence reads, 'drive him away, for he is not thy son, he is not born to thee', and the remainder of the sentence is marked as unintelligible.[3] In the writings of the same sage it is stated that he who transgresses the ordinances of Maat (Maet, that is, of personified right, order, truth) will be punished.[4] But the thought seems to be, not that the punishment will come by a personal act of deity, but by the working of the ordered laws that govern the universe. This point of view may be illustrated by the following text: My heart 'was an excellent prompter unto me; I did not infringe its commands; I feared to transgress its guidance. Therefore I prospered exceedingly, and was fortunate on account of that which it caused me to do; I succeeded by reason of its guidance. Of a sooth, true is that which is said by men: "It [the heart] is the voice of God that is in every body; happy is he whom it has led to a good course of action" [5].' By acting in accordance with right reason, for the heart with the Egyptians as with the Hebrews was the seat of intellect, he kept his life in harmony with the due order of the world in general and of human society in particular and hence enjoyed prosperity and happiness. For the Egyptian had little or no conception of wrong-doing as a personal offence against the divinity. To quote H. Frankfort: 'There are many Egyptian words to denote evil acts, but I doubt whether any should be rendered by "sin", if one grants that word its proper theological connotation '.[6]

Sickness was attributed to the activity of demons or spirits. 'Illness was thought to be due to the presence of haunting

[1] A. Erman, *The Literature of the Ancient Egyptians*, trans. by A. M. Blackman (London 1927) 307
[2] Sir E. A. Wallis Budge, *The Teaching of Amen-em-apt* (London 1924) 9
[3] Erman-Blackman, *op. cit.*, p. 59
[4] H. Frankfort, *Ancient Egyptian Religion* (New York 1948) 62; Erman-Blackman, *op. cit.*, p. 57
[5] Quoted by Sir Alan H. Gardiner in ERE V 475*b*
[6] H. Frankfort, *op. cit.*, p. 73

spirits of the dead'.[1] Disease 'was always regarded as the work of demons, spirits . . . or spirits of the dead'.[2] Yet there are one or two exceptional texts in which the sufferer attributes his malady to wrong-doing. One such sufferer was Neferabu (Nofriabu), a worker in the necropolis at Deir el-Medineh, whom P. Virey describes as a publican among the Pharisees, 'who once in his life had the extraordinary idea of accusing and humiliating himself'.[3] The text begins: 'I was an ignorant man and without understanding, unable to distinguish good from evil'. But the experts differ as to the interpretation. In the opinion of H. Frankfort the text illustrates the truth that 'the theme of God's wrath is practically unknown in Egyptian literature; for the Egyptian, in his aberrations, is not a sinner whom God rejects but an ignorant man who is disciplined and corrected'.[4] J. Vandier, however, sees in the text a sign of moral development and the recognition of sin. The suppliant 'established between the sin and the chastisement the relation of cause and effect'. And Vandier attributes this new conception to the influence of Semitic strangers amomg the workers in the necropolis.[5] So, even if this view were admitted to be correct, the text would not indicate more than a local moral progress among a class of workers.

Such self-accusation was extremely rare. In most cases the Egyptian proclaims his entire innocence and life-long adherence to all the precepts of sound morality. Hence the name of 'ideal biographies' given to the funerary inscriptions. Even in the *Book of the Dead* the dead man before the tribunal of Osiris has no single fault to admit. His protestation of innocence is given in the so-called 'Negative Confession' contained in the 125th chapter of that work, copies of which were buried with the dead. There must originally have been a conception of a real judgment to be faced in the underworld, but this was overlaid with ideas of the potency of magical

[1] A. H. Gardiner, ERE V 476*a*
[2] G. Foucart, ERE IV 750*a*
[3] P. Virey, *La Religion de l'ancienne Égypte* (Paris 1910) 65
[4] H. Frankfort, *op. cit.*, p. 77
[5] J. Vandier, *La religion égyptienne* (Paris 1944) 221

formulas by the knowledge of which the departed can escape any of the many dangers otherwise threatening the souls of the departed. There is nothing of religious sentiment or devotion in this work. Neither is there any sincere recognition of the moral obligation to do good and avoid evil, though the ethical standard each avers himself to have maintained consistently throughout life, is lofty and noble. The *Book of the Dead* is a magical composition, known to us first in a text of the second millennium but containing essential elements dating from the third. So early did true religion tend to become dominated by magical conceptions.

Greek religious thought and practice had this in common with Egyptian religion that in the course of a long history new ideas and rites were introduced. There was no official body to regulate belief and the way was always open for the infiltration of foreign deities and their worship. Poets and philosophers with their varied outlook exercised their influence on wider and narrower circles ; and the Orphic and Eleusinian Mysteries won large numbers of adherents. As a result it is not possible to give a simple clear-cut account of Greek religion valid for all classes and for all periods of its history. Yet the Olympian system of the gods as found in Homer never lost its hold on the people as a whole and constituted a stable element. But like the Egyptian the Greek religion presents incongruous elements. And this is so even with regard to the particular problem that occupies us here. In the first place though the gods were thought to punish wrongdoing, they themselves were not conceived as above the moral weaknesses of mortals. Thus the noble-minded Aeschylus, so concerned to justify the ways of the gods to men, represents Zeus, the usurper of the throne of his father Ouranos, as harsh in his dealings. And he explains that such is the characteristic of all who are new to power.[1] The gods were, in the main, men writ large. And the evil the gods were thought to punish consisted largely in violations of divine rights committed by neglect of the due observance of their ceremonies or as invasions of their prerogatives by unbroken prosperity and excessive self-exaltation. Thus

[1] *Prometheus*, 35 : *ἅπας δὲ τραχὺς ὅστις ἂν νέον κρατῇ.*

Herodotus writes that nemesis fell on Croesus 'as may be supposed, because he thought of himself as the happiest of men'.[1] And the reason alleged why the constant success of mere mortals is said to bring disaster is the ignoble passion of jealousy harboured by the gods.[2] This spirit is strikingly illustrated in the story of Prometheus. The offence charged against him was that he stole fire, the treasured possession of Hephaestus and the gods, and bestowed the benefit of its use on mortal men. For this benevolent crime he was sentenced by Zeus to be clamped to a desolate crag by the ocean in the wilds of Scythia. Such beliefs were not of a nature to inspire men with profound reverence and love of the divinity.

Moreover, the Greeks never formed a clear conception of sin both as a violation of a divine command and therefore as an affront to divinity, and as a moral degradation of the soul. Wrongdoing was rather a violation of right order that tended to bring its own retribution. This could be attributed to Fate. The ancient teaching, as Aeschylus puts it in the mouth of a chorus, was that the perpetrator of evil must suffer 'as the thrice-aged maxim words it'.[3] But there was no clear satisfactory conciliation of the operation of Fate and the government of the gods. Not only man but the gods themselves were subject to the inexorable decrees of Fate. So the Pythian oracle proclaimed in answer to Croesus: 'Destined Fate not even a god can escape'.[4] An attempt was, however, made, as by Aeschylus, to reduce Fate to a function of Zeus. But this harmonisation does not seem to have won wide acceptance. There was, therefore, an inner tension between the two concepts. On the one hand the web of man's destiny was woven for him at birth, a task attributed to the three personified Fates. According to a line of Hesiod's, 'They allot to man at birth to have good and to have evil'. This, therefore, before the possibility of any transgression. Yet the poet proceeds, 'They pursue the transgressions both of gods

[1] Herodotus i. 34: *ὡς εἰκάσαι, ὅτι ἐνόμισε ἑωυτὸν εἶναι ἀνθρώπων ἁπάντων ὀλβιώτατον.*

[2] Herodotus iii. 40: *τὸ θεῖον ἐπισταμένῳ ὡς ἔστι φθονερόν.*

[3] Choephoroi, 313f.: *δράσαντι παθεῖν, τριγέρων μῦθος τάδε φωνεῖ.*

[4] Herodotus i. 91: *τὴν πεπρωμένην μοῖραν ἀδύνατά ἐστι ἀποφυγέειν καὶ θεῷ.*

and of men, nor do (these) goddesses ever cease from their dread wrath till with a visitation of evil they requite whoso has sinned '.[1]

Still, the experience of the Greeks, as of other nations, showed that often there is no apparent relation between the moral qualities of men and the prosperity they enjoy. So Solon writes :

> Many are rich but wicked, good but poor,
> Yet will we not give these in exchange
> Wealth in place of virtue. For this abideth ever,
> But riches are now of one, now of another.[2]

And Theognis complains of this apparent injustice :

> And this, O king of the immortals, how is it just,
> That a man alien from works unjust,
> Innocent of transgression or sinful oath,
> But living in justice, does not experience what is just ?
> What other mortal, seeing this, would then
> Revere the gods ? [3]

So the problem of undeserved suffering pressed on reflective minds and even led to a disparagement of the gods. But probably in the mass of men it did not arouse distressing thoughts. They would take the world as they found it and endeavour to make the best of it, perhaps with the reflection that when Fate has decreed, it is useless to repine. The Orphic and Eleusinian Mysteries introduced new beliefs concerning

[1] Hesiod, *Theogonia*, 218–222

[2] Solon, *Poetae Gnomici Graeci* (1823) 98f. :

> Πολλοὶ γὰρ πλουτεῦσι κακοί, ἀγαθοὶ δὲ πένονται.
> Αλλ'ἡμεῖς αὖτοῖς οὐ διαμευψόμεθα
> Τῆς ἀρετῆς τὸν πλοῦτον· ἐπεὶ τὸ μὲν ἔμπεδον αἰεί,
> Χρήματα δ'ἀνθρώπων ἄλλοτε ἄλλος ἔχει.

[3] Theognis, 743–9

> Καὶ τοῦτ', ἀθανάτων βασιλεῦ, πῶς ἐστὶ δίκαιον
> Εργων ὅστις ἀνὴρ ἐκτὸς ἐὼν ἀδίκων,
> Μή τιν' ὑπερβασίην κατέχων μήθ' ὅρκον ἀλιτρὸν
> Αλλὰ δίκαιος ἐών, μὴ τὰ δίκαια παθεῖν ;
> Τίς δή κεν βρότος ἄλλος, ὁρῶν πρὸς τοῦτον, ἔπειτα
> Αζοιτ' ἀθανάτους;

life after death which would provide a corrective for the apparently haphazard distribution of human fortunes in this life. But for the people at large the Homeric conception of Hades offered nothing attractive, nothing to compensate for the inequalities of life. Hades was the abode of the dead in general where the shades passed a dull and dismal existence, while the wicked suffered in Tartaros.

The more lofty minds will have recognised the educative and moral value of suffering. It teaches man his insufficiency, his powerlessness to work his own will, and saves him from the *hubris*, the arrogant overbearing frame of mind that arises from the consciousness of strength and power and is so hateful to gods and men. This truth is put by Aeschylus into the mouth of the chorus in the Agamennon. They say that Zeus has laid it down as an established law that suffering is the road to wisdom.[1] So also Croesus according to the story in Herodotus says to Cyrus : 'My sufferings, unpleasant as they are, have turned out to be instructions'.[2]

The Romans on this subject had little or nothing to add to the conceptions of the Greeks. They thought of Orcus, the abode of the Manes or departed shades, much as the Greeks did of Hades. Their pantheon resembled that of the Greeks and was in large measure identified with it. And like the Greeks they admitted in course of time various foreign cults and also philosophies. Chief among these in connection with suffering is the system of the Stoics. And from the pen of Lucius Annaeus Seneca, one of the most distinguished Roman representatives of the school, we are fortunate to possess a treatise on this very subject *De Mundi Gubernatione et Divina Providentia.* It was written in answer to a question from his friend Lucilius 'why it is that, if the world is ruled by providence, many evils befall good men'. He answers that God acts towards the good man like a good father. 'He tests, hardens, prepares him for Himself'. He goes so far as to say that 'nothing evil can befall a good man ; contraries do not mix together'. Just as all the fresh water that rivers pour into the sea is changed into the

[1] Agamemnon, 177f. : *τὸν πάθει μάθος θέντα κυρίως ἔχειν.*

[2] Herodotus i. 207 : *τὰ δέ μοι παθήματα ἐόντα ἀχάριτα μαθήματα γεγόνεε.*

quality that characterises the ocean, so the strong man 'assumes whatever happens into his own characteristics'. It is not that he does not feel; he feels but overcomes. 'Adversity of every kind he regards as an opportunity of exerting himself', like an athlete who takes every occasion to strengthen his muscles. 'Virtue tends to wilt without something to struggle against'. God who is full of love for the good ('bonorum amantissimus') tries them with labours, sufferings, and loss. Misfortunes are of advantage to those who endure them just as it is to submit to the surgeon's knife. 'Calamity is virtue's opportunity'. God tries the best with bad health, grief, or troubles, just as in war the general entrusts dangerous enterprises to the bravest. So when we have to suffer, we should say 'God has deemed us worthy of the test how much human nature can endure'. As everything that exceeds the mean is harmful, there is great danger in protracted prosperity. 'The gods follow the same line of action with good men as do teachers with their pupils; the more certain the hope of success, the more work they demand of them'. 'As gold is tested by fire, so brave men by misery'.

Thus Seneca has put on record many noble sentiments nobly expressed and many of his thoughts can be of use to Christians if understood in a Christian spirit, for the source of these sentiments is purely human and self-regarding. In fact, it is not going beyond the truth to assert that this philosophy springs from human self-sufficiency. The proud, self-reliant man is unwilling to yield to opposition, whether it comes from men or from circumstances. He will be master of the situation, if that is by any means possible. One way of rising superior to the blows of misfortune is to avoid repining and self-pity, and to treat them as beneficial and as if willed by oneself. This eliminates the feeling of being forced to submit to what is imposed from without. It is a form of autarchy. So far does Seneca carry this spirit that he says in so many words: 'I am under no compulsion; I suffer nothing against my will. Neither do I submit to the will of God; I am in agreement with it'.[1] And again: 'Endure bravely. In this

[1] 'Nihil cogor, nihil patior invitus; nec servio Deo, sed assentior'.

way you surpass God, for He has no part in bearing ills, whereas you stand superior to endurance '.[1] A further grave evil that infects the system and also has its roots in the striving for human self-sufficiency is the glorification of suicide. The brave man, says Seneca, always has a way out, if and when he desires. The taking of his own life is considered a manifestation of his bravery. This is an arrogation to man of the right to determine the issue of life, a right which God has reserved to Himself.

The beliefs of the Babylonians have a special interest and importance in connection with our present subject on account of their racial and environmental affinity to the Hebrews, and for that reason some account of them may be conveniently reserved to the next chapter.

More detailed bibliographies may be found in the following. Brahmanism—A. Roussel, ' Religions de l'Inde ', DAFC II 645–76 ; L. de la Vallée Poussin, ' Karma ', ERE ' VII 673–6 ; E. R. Hull, S.J., *Hinduism* in *Lectures* (CTS).

Buddhism—A. A. Macdonell, ' Indian Buddhism ', ERE VI 209–16 ; L. de la Vallée Poussin, ' Bouddhisme et religions de l'Inde ' in Huby, *Christus*, 220–97, also *Buddhism* in *Lectures* (CTS).

Kabbalists—M. Gaster, ' Transmigration (Jewish) ', ERE XII 435–40.

Iranian Religion—L. C. Casartelli, ' Iranian Dualism ', ERE V 111–12, also *The Great Kings* in *Lectures* (CTS) ; A. J. Carnoy, ' Zoroastrianism ', ERE XII 862–8, also ' La religion des Perses ' in Huby, *Christus*, 161–219, also *The Avesta* in *Lectures* (CTS).

For the Egyptian religion see the works cited in the notes.

For Greek and Roman religion : P. D. Chantepie de la Saussaye, *Lehrbuch der Religiongeschichte* (Freiburg i.B. 1897, vol. II) ; J. E. Harrison, *Prolegomena to the Study of Greek Religion* (Cambridge 1903) ; W. Warde Fowler, *The Religious*

[1] ' Ferte fortiter ; hoc est quo Deum antecedatis. Ille extra patientiam malorum est, vos supra patientiam '.

Experience of the Roman People (London 1911); F. Altheim, *A History of Roman Religion* (English trans. by H. Mattingly; London 1938); L. R. Farnell, 'Greek Religion' in ERE; also articles, *ibid.*, 'Ethics and Morality', 'Eschatology'; 'Fate'; 'Abode of the Blest'; 'Under World'.

Chapter II

THE RELIGION OF THE BABYLONIANS

Our subject does not call for a complete account of the religion of the Babylonians and Assyrians but only for certain aspects which help to illustrate it whether by similitude or contrast.

The most fundamental difference between this religion and that of the Israelites is that between polytheism and monotheism. The Babylonians—for convenience this name may for our present purpose be used with occasional exception to cover both the Babylonians and the Assyrians—had a very large pantheon. The number of the gods ran into many hundreds. This multiplicity had its origin in part in the composite nature of the religion which, like that of Egypt, resulted from the fusion of various local cults. In the early stages of their history the various cities formed sovereign independent states as they did also in Greece. As they became politically unified, so also the gods of the different cities found their place in a pantheon common to the whole country. In the course of this process certain gods with similar attributes and functions came to be identified. And this assimilation led to a blurring of the characters of certain divinities. The reason of this was that the attributes and functions of gods eventually identified varied in the cities which were their original homes, the population of one ascribing wider attributes to a god than the population of another, where some of these same functions were ascribed to another god.

These divinities were not conceived as eternal and uncreated. According to *Enuma elish* the primeval couple Apsu and Tiamat were the progenitors of Lahmu and Lahamu. Then in turn Anshar and Kishar were born. Anshar was the father of Anu, who became the great god of heaven, and Anu of Nudimmud. Thus the host of heaven gradually came into existence. But there was no uniform belief in this matter of theogony. Supremacy in the pantheon tended to be the prerogative of the god specially honoured in the particular city which attained political pre-eminence. Thus in an Assyrian cosmogony Ashur, the great national god of Assyria, is called his own creator and father of the gods.[1]

Further, though the gods were considered to be immortal, this prerogative did not protect them against being deprived of existence. Apsu, though the first progenitor of the gods, was put to death by Ea. He first by means of an incantation caused Apsu to fall asleep, then broke his muscles, tore away his crown, chained and finally slew him.[2] Later after a terrific encounter Marduk destroyed Tiamat, the primeval consort of Apsu. The conqueror's arrow passed through Tiamat's wide-open mouth and wounded her in the belly. He cut her entrails, cleaved her heart, and, having chained her, deprived her of life.[3] The details of these accounts help us to comprehend the Babylonian conception of divine beings. We should be far from the mark if we gave to the word 'divinity' as applied to a member of the pantheon anything like the connotation now associated with it in our minds. When the Flood broke on the earth, the gods were stricken with terror and fled up to heaven 'cowering like curs'. And when after the Flood had abated, Uta-napishtim offered a sacrifice, the gods smelt the sweet savour and assembled like flies over the offering.[4] It is clear that such deities could not inspire in their worshippers the sentiments of reverence entertained by pious Israelites towards the one God who created heaven and earth by His mere word, who had no consort and no offspring like the pagan gods, but who in His transcendent majesty condescended to treat men as their father and to allow them to think and speak of Him accordingly. None the less beside these crude texts elevated and dignified passages are found not only in the hymns and prayers but also in the incantation formulas.

Shamash, the sun-god, was held to be the upholder of

[1] Dhorme, *Choix*, 92
[2] *Enuma elish* I 60–9
[3] *Enuma elish* IV 93–103
[4] *Epic of Gilgamesh* XI 113–15 ; 160. (Thompson, *Epic*, 52f. ; Dhorme, *Choix*, 111, 115 ; Pritchard, *Texts*, 94f.)

justice. One of his sons, a personification of virtue, was named Kettu 'Justice', and another similarly Mēsharu 'Rectitude' or 'Righteousness'. Shamash presumably owed this moral character to his ubiquitous presence. His eye shining in every part of the world, he necessarily knows all the actions of men. A long hymn addressed to him is full of his praise. He knows the designs of men; he watches their footsteps. He hates the breaking of oaths, the violation of other men's marriage rights, unjust judgments, the taking of bribes, unjust weights and measures, mouths full of lying. All guilty of such iniquities Shamash visits with punishment. The horn of the wicked is destroyed; his dwelling is overturned; his seed has no continuance. Those who practise the opposite virtues enjoy the blessings of Shamash. Their life is prolonged; their abode is enriched, their family is enlarged. In the forefront of those who appeal to him are the weak, the poor, the afflicted, those in danger.[1] On the other hand, a hymn to Ishtar lauds her for her endowment of 'vitality, charm, and voluptuousness', a combination of qualities foreign to our conception of the divine. And these words of praise occur twice in the hymn.[2] Another hymn to the same goddess, this time as patron of war, speaks of her as causing peaceable brothers to fight, but later praises her regard for the oppressed and ill-treated.[3] A hymn to Sin, the moon-god, attributes to him the encouragement of truth and justice.[4] The ethical element, however, is not prominent in the hymns.

The noblest sentiments to be found in Babylonian literature occur in a text that may be classed as Wisdom Literature and recalls the biblical book of Proverbs. The following lines are not all consecutive in the original.

> Against thine opponent work no evil.
> Whoso does evil, reward him with good.
> Treat thine enemy with justice.

[1] A. Jeremias in ERE V 445; F. J. Stephens, more fully and in the light of more recent research, in Pritchard, *Texts*, 387–9

[2] F. J. Stephens in Pritchard, *Texts*, 383

[3] F. J. Stephens in Pritchard, *Texts*, 384

[4] Gressmann, *Texte*, 242; Pritchard, *Texts*, 386

Give bread to eat ; give wine to drink.
Whoso begs an alms, respect and clothe him ;
Thereat his god rejoices ;
That is pleasing to Shamash ; he rewards it with good.
Give help ; do good always and ever.
Slander not ; speak what is noble ;
Say naught of evil ; let thy talk be good.
Whoso slanders, whoso speaks evil,
In retribution Shamash watches for his head.
Open not wide thy mouth ; keep guard over thy lips ;
A hasty speech thou wilt later regret.
Reverence begets prosperity ;
Sacrifice lengthens life
And prayer remits (the punishment of) sin.[1]

These are unquestionably noble thoughts and precepts, and recall those of the Gospel. To what extent was this lofty teaching reflected in the lives of the people ? To what extent was it only the ideal of a reflective religious mind ? A. Jeremias remarks that 'we are unable to say whether the elevated morality presupposed by the injunctions of the priests was ever actually practised by any class of the people', and in his opinion 'there existed a . . . discrepancy between theory and practice'.[2] This latter remark taken alone would be true of all religions. Of no religion can it be said that there is complete harmony between the lives of its adherents and its moral teachings. Jeremias clearly means that the evidence points to the conclusion that there was no serious effort in any section of the population to reduce this lofty code of morality to practice.

Further evidence of the code of morality and the conception of sin prevalent among the Babylonians is to be found in the incantation texts, which form a large part of the extant literature. They believed that one of the chief causes of the

[1] Quoted partially by A. Condamin in Huby, *Christus*, 531 f., and by A. Jeremias in ERE V 446*a*, at length by E. Ebeling in Gressmann, *Texte*, 291-3, and R. H. Pfeiffer in Pritchard, *Texts*, 426f.

[2] ERE V 445*a*

evils that befall mankind was the wrath of the gods. Sickness and other troubles could also be inflicted by malign spirits and through the magical powers of witches and wizards. Or trouble might be due merely to the superior strength of one god over another. This would explain defeat at the hands of a hostile army, the patron god of the victorious state proving stronger than the god of his enemies. This was believed to have been the case when Urukagina, the *isag* or king of Lagash, who had been an upholder of justice by protecting the poor and weak from oppression and extortion, suffered defeat and overthrow at the hands of Lugalzaggisi, the ruler of neighbouring Umma. The writer of the tablet recording the ruthless sacking of the shrines of Lagash 'can find no reason for the wrongs the city has suffered in any transgression on the part of Urukagina, its king ; for Ningirsu [the patron-god of Lagash] has had no cause to be angry with his representative. All he can do is to protest his belief that the city-god will one day be avenged upon the men of Umma and their goddess Nidaba'.[1] In most instances, however, afflictions were thought to be due to one of the other causes, either the anger of a deity or some malign influence.

An offended god might withdraw his protecting hand and allow the victim of his wrath to pass under the power of some one or more of the numerous evil spirits. And the incantation formulas, some of which contain no reference to previous wrongdoing, suggest that the sickness or other trouble might be due to the direct action of some malign spirit. In either case the spirits could be exorcised by the priests, a special class of whom was entrusted with this function. The *mashmashu* or *āshipu*, as the exorcising priest was called, accompanied the recitation of the incantation formula with various magical rites. Thus, if the malady from which the suppliant was suffering was suspected to be due to a witch or wizard, a representation of the supposed sorcerer was used and by virtue

[1] L. W. King, *A History of Sumer and Akka*, (London 1910) 191 and on the history of Urukagina, 176–91 ; briefly in H. R. Hall, *The Ancient History of the Near East* (London 1950[11]), 182f. ; Sumerian text with German translation in F. Thureau-Dangin, *Die sumerischen und akkadischen Königinschriften* (Leipzig 1907) ; Vorderasiatische Bibliothek I i) 56–8

of the incantation the sufferings of the victim were transferred by means of the image to their originator. These incantation texts did not neglect also to appeal to the help of the gods. It was the superior knowledge of the priest that enabled him to choose the formula rightly applicable to the case of the sufferer.[1]

In order that the actual cause of the affliction and the god or goddess actually offended might be duly named in the incantation a long list of deities might be invoked and a long list of possible transgressions enumerated. This is well illustrated by a long text of nearly two hundred lines, of which the following are non-continuous extracts. The text is important as showing the recognised standards of morality.

Has he offended his god, offended his goddess ?
Has he refused instead of agreeing ?
Has he agreed instead of refusing ?
Has he slighted his goddess ?
Has he spoken evil ?
Has he estranged father and son,
Estranged son and father,
Estranged mother and daughter,
Estranged daughter and mother,
Estranged mother-in-law and daughter-in-law,
Estranged daughter-in-law and mother-in-law,
Estranged brother and brother,
Estranged friend and friend,
Estranged companion and companion ?
Has he not let a captive go free,
Not allowed a prisoner to see the light of day ?
Has he sinned against a god,
Committed an offence against a goddess ?
Has he wronged a god,
Slighted a goddess ?
Is there an offence against his god,
A fault against his goddess ?
Is there hatred against his elder brother ?

[1] Jastrow, *Religion*, 270–91, 307f., gives a number of such texts.

Has he slighted father or mother,
Wronged his elder sister ?
Has he said 'Yes' for 'No',
'No' for 'Yes'?
Has he used a false balance,
Taken false money,
Not given true money ?
Has he disinherited a rightful son,
Established an illegitimate son ?
Has he marked boundaries falsely,
Not had boundaries rightly marked ?
Has he intruded upon the house of his neighbour ?
Has he approached his neighbour's wife ?
Has he shed his neighbour's blood ?
Has he robbed his neighbour's garments ?
Has he not let a man out of his power ?
Has he driven a worthy man from his family ?
Has he broken up well-united kindred ?
Has he risen up against one in authority ?
Was his mouth upright, his heart false,
His mouth full of consent, his heart of refusal ?
Has he busied himself with magic and sorcery ?
Is it because of grievous wrong that he has done,
On account of the many sins that he has committed ?
Has he promised with heart and mouth, and not fulfilled,
Through a gift [withheld] contemned the name of his god,
Consecrated something but held it back ?
Has he risen in an assembly and spoken what is harmful ?
Whatever charm has fallen on him, may it be broken !

Then follows a list of the possible causes of the charm or enchantment that has overpowered him. (Through a misunderstanding of the German verb 'bannen' which means both *to banish* and *to enchant* one English translation here speaks in terms of *outlawry*).

Has he worked mischief against his city ?
Has he impaired the fame of his city ?

Here follows the invocation of Shamash, of Nergal, of Anu and Anatu, and of many other gods and goddesses calling upon them to break the charm and free the sufferer from his afflictions. Finally may be quoted the lines:

> May the stars of South, North, East, and West,
> May the four winds blow and break the charm ![1]

It will be noticed that there is no expression of sorrow for sin committed and no expression of determination to avoid it in the future. There is no regret for having committed an offence against the gods precisely as such an offence. The only idea stressed is that such an offence incurs the displeasure of the gods and calls down punishment. Perhaps it is out of place to look for such expressions of sorrow and purpose of amendment, for the suppliant does not in fact accuse himself of any particular wrongdoing. 'There is no question of retribution for actual acts of injustice or violence, any more than there is a question of genuine contrition. The enumeration of the causes for the suffering constitutes in fact a part of the incantation. The mention of the real cause in the long list—and the list aims to be exhaustive, so that the exorciser may strike the real cause—goes a long way towards ensuring the departure of the evil spirit'.[2] Not only real transgressions against the moral code are enumerated in these documents but also mere unconscious slips in the celebration of ritual; and no distinction is drawn between the two classes of wrongful action. Both are equally potent in arousing indignation in the gods. There is further a danger of our reading into the texts more elevated sentiments than actually moved the suppliants. The occasion of this misunderstanding arises from the fact that the same word hîtu or hittu means *sin*, *guilt*, and *punishment*, which is the result of sin, and similarly the one word *shertu* means *anger*, also the *punishment* which anger inflicts, and also

[1] H. Zimmern, *Beiträge zur Kenntnis der babylonischen Religion: die Beschwörungstafeln Shurpu* (Leipzig 1901) 2–11; partial translations in Jastrow, *Religion*, 291; by A. Condamin in Huby, *Christus*, 529f.; A. Jeremias in ERE V 446*b*

[2] Jastrow, *Religion*, 292

sin or *iniquity*, which is the cause of the anger. Thus in a text which can be translated ' Cleanse me from my sin ' it is very probable, to judge by the tone of these prayers as a whole, that the petition is not for purity of conscience but for liberation from the affliction or suffering thought to be the consequence of guilt.

So strong was this conviction of the relation between suffering and transgression that a suppliant would pray for the appeasement of divine wrath even while proclaiming his ignorance what god or goddess he might have offended or what he might have done to arouse such indignation against himself.

May the wrath of my lord's heart be mollified !
May the god I know not, be mollified !
May the goddess I know not, be mollified !
May the known god and the unknown be mollified !
May the known goddess and the unknown be mollified !

Then after other similar prayers :

The offence I have committed I know not ;
The sin I have sinned I know not.

There follow petitions for a gracious reception of his supplication and then the sufferer continues :

Pure food I have not eaten ;
Clear water I have not drunk.

Whether these words express the spirit of penance in which the prayer is offered or the state of suffering to which the suppliant is reduced, is not clear. Although ignorant of any specific transgression to which his condition could be traced, he freely acknowledges his manifold guilt.

O lord ! my offences are many ; great are my sins.
O god ! my offences are many ; great are my sins.
My goddess ! my offences are many ; great are my sins.

Known god and unknown! my offences are many; great
 are my sins.
The offence I have committed I know not;
The sin I have sinned I know not.

The next line seems to say:

Suffering became my food, I know not why.

This militates against the interpretation of the previous reference to fasting as an act of penance. Of the remainder of the prayer it may suffice to quote the following three lines:

The lord in the wrath of his heart has looked upon me.
The sin I have sinned turn to favour——!
The offence I have committed, may the wind bear away![1]

In this psalm there is no trace of any resentment or of any questioning of the justice of the suffering endured. The suppliant seems content with the conviction that specific cause there must have been, although its precise nature was hidden from him, and with the reflection that in any case his transgressions and sins in the past have been both numerous and great. Not all sufferers, however, accepted their lot in this spirit.

In a poem known under the title 'I will praise the Lord of Wisdom' the speaker complains bitterly that the gravity of his afflictions shows that he is being treated as if he were a wrong-doer and that it is impossible for ordinary mortals to fathom the designs of the gods. In the end, however, he is restored to health and strength by the great god Marduk, but no explanation is offered of his previous suffering nor of the motives that led to the divine intervention on his behalf.

The day is misery, the night weeping;
The month is silence, sorrow the year.

[1] H. Zimmern, *Babylonische Busspsalmen* (Leipzig 1885) 64–6; partial translation in Jastrow, *Religion*, 320–2

Like a dove bemoan I all my days.
Turn where I will, there is evil and more evil ;
My misfortunes increase ; right do I not find.
To my god I called, he vouchsafed not his countenance ;
I prayed to my goddess, she raised not her head.

The interpreters neither of omens nor of dreams could explain the state of affairs. The neocromancer could not help ; the exorciser could effect no release from the wrath heavy on the sufferer. He was

Like one who had not offered a libation to a god
And at a meal had not invoked a goddess,
Had not bowed his head, had known no reverence,
In whose mouth intercession and prayer had ceased,
Who had not taught his people reverence and awe,
Like one who by his majestic god had lightly sworn—such was I !
Whereas my thoughts had been of intercession and supplication.
Supplication was my rule, sacrifice my order.
The day gods are worshipped was the joy of my heart ;
The day of the procession of the goddess was gain for me and riches.
I taught my land to observe the divine precepts ;
I brought my people to honour the name of the goddess.
What man thinks good, for god is evil !
What in his heart is wrong, for his god is good !
Who can learn the will of the gods in heaven ?
Where has purblind man learnt the way of a god ?
The living man of yesterday is dead today.
Quickly comes gloom ; speedily is he crushed.
One moment he sings a song of triumph,
The next he wails like a mourner.

In badly preserved lines, after a break in the tablet, the complaint goes on to say that a shade of the dead has come from the abyss bringing (?) pains in the head from the underworld.

The evil spirits (?) have sprained his sinews, dislocated his neck, brought on trembling, caused burning fever. Some demon has taken possession of his body like a garment. He cannot see ; he cannot hear. His hands are weak ; his knees are feeble. Bread he cannot eat ; beer he cannot drink. Long has lasted this languishing. Through hunger his flesh falls away. His bed is his prison. He has no rest nor breathing-space day or night. After some unpleasant details of what has happened to him through his extremity of exhaustion, he repeats that exorcist and reader of omens were powerless to help.

No god helped nor clasped my hand ;
No goddess in pity came to my side.
The grave was open ; men took my possessions.
Before I was dead, the weeping for me ended.
My enemy heard of it and his features brightened ;
The woman that hated me, was told of it and her heart rejoiced.
But I know the day when my tears come to an end,
When among the protecting deities their divinity will have mercy.

This unexpected outburst of confidence following on such a delineation of such apparently hopeless misery is most striking. The supreme confidence of Job springs inevitably to mind.[1]

The third and last tablet of this poem opens with the description of two dreams, the text of which is regrettably badly preserved. In each a figure appears, both sent by the gods. In the second vision the messenger proclaims that his mission is to secure propitiation for the sufferer. There follow further rather obscure references to a heavenly visitant and another dream, and then :

After the heart of the lord was appeased,
And the liver of merciful Marduk was soothed.

[1] Job 19:23–7

At this point there is a gap of eight lines ; then :

> He caused the wind to take away my transgressions.

He sent off the malign wind to its store-house on the horizon where the firmament meets the earth—such appears to be the meaning ; he dismissed the vile shade or ghost and dispatched the demons to the underworld. The feverish shivering is drowned in the sea ; the root of weakness is torn out ; trouble with eyes and ears is ended. The various members of the body, enumerated one by one, are restored to health. Then Marduk took the sufferer's hand and lifted his head high.

Now, once more in good health, with prayer and downcast eyes he enters Esagila, Marduk's temple at Babylon, offers incense, rich gifts and sacrifices. And so the poem is rounded off with praise of Marduk and his consort Sarpanitum.[1]

Thus the story with its happy ending makes manifest the kindly disposition of the gods, but makes no attempt to solve the theological problem presented by the sufferer's grievous afflictions.

Another interesting text dealing with the same theme is a dialogue, which has been variously named 'The Babylonian Theodicy' and 'A Dialogue about Human Misery'. The original poem, which does not equal the poetic power of that just discussed, was in twenty-seven strophes, each of eleven lines. It has the peculiarity of being an acrostic, each line of each strophe beginning with the same letter or syllable. As interpreted by B. Landsberger, this acrostic reads : 'I, Shaggil-kinam-ubbib, the exorcist, honour god and king'. The text, which is badly preserved, is of uncertain date, being adjudged by different scholars to the second and to the first millennium B.C. On account of the ravages of time it is not possible to give a coherent reproduction of the thread of the argument.

[1] Translations by E. Ebeling in Gressmann, *Texte*, 273–81 and by R. H. Pfeiffer in Pritchard, *Texts*, 434–7. Partial translations by R. Campbell Thompson in *Proceedings of the Society of Biblical Archaeology* 32 (1910) 18–24 and R. W. Rogers, *Cuneiform Parallels to the Old Testament* (Oxford 1912) 164–9. J. Nougayrol, 'Une version ancienne du "Juste Souffrant"', RB 59 (1952) 239–50. Text in transcription with translation in S. Landersdorfer, O.S.B., *Eine babylonische Quelle für das Buch Job ?* (Freiburg im Breisgau 1911 ;=Biblische Studian XVI ii)

The sufferer opens the debate.[1] I. He seeks consolation and wishes to tell the story of his afflictions to a sympathetic friend. He has lost his father and mother, and is now alone. II. F. (Do not take your personal troubles too much to heart as if your lot was different from that of other men.) All men go the way of death; every man must cross the river of the nether world. (If a man is prosperous, he owes it to his religious spirit, for) only the devout enjoy the protection of heaven. III. S. His store of provisions is exhausted and he suffers want. His strength is vanishing. (Is there any sign of divine protection in such conditions?) IV. F. (The sufferer is wrong in his way of speaking.) He must pray to (the angered) god. So may he obtain favour and forgiveness. V. S. Consider the wild ass and the fierce lion. (They have their freedom and all their needs are met.) But have they troubled themselves about the worship of the gods? And has every rich and arrogant man paid due worship to the gods? But for my part I never neglected prayer nor due offerings. VI. F. The counsel of the gods is indeed inscrutable. The wild ass is blameless, but in the end he meets with an arrow. The lion, enemy of flocks, falls into the open pit. The wealthy upstart meets with an untimely death at the hands of the king. No, their lot is not enviable. Better to seek the favour of the gods. VII. S. The friend gives wise counsel; but the fact remains:

> They go by the path of prosperity who seek not god;
> They become impoverished and enfeebled who supplicate the goddess.

(His own experience proves it.) From his earliest years he has sought the will of the god; he has been humbly devout to his goddess. Yet in return he receives not wealth but want. VIII. F. The sufferer is rejecting the truth and mocking at the divine ordinance. He desires to neglect the cult of the gods. Like the inmost heaven itself the counsel of the gods is un-

[1] The Roman numerals introduce the new strophes. The letters 'S' and 'F' introduce respectively the reflections of the sufferer and of his friend. Round brackets contain sentences which are not in the original text but seem to indicate the line of thought.

fathomable. It is beyond the capabilities of man to attain understanding thereof.[1]

XII. F. (The friend appeals to the lesson of his own case. If things go well with him, it is because) he fulfils all his duties, household and religious. XIII. S. (So far from being convinced by this argument) the sufferer has decided to leave his house (and household duties) and not to bother about religious ceremonies. (He will act like the wild beasts he has praised and) will lead a free life in the open, finding his food as he can. XIV. F. (An endeavour to persuade the sufferer to abandon this plan of) abandoning ordinary human activity. XV. S. (No, he is determined to live among and like) the beasts of the fields. XVI. F. [Only polite introductory words are preserved.] XVII. S. Life among men is too unstable; there are so many strange reversals of fortune. XVIII. F. (An effort to bring the sufferer to a better frame of mind by recalling that) the devout man prospers and has the wherewithal to be liberal to others. XIX. S. He has sought wisdom, studied the tablets, but found no happiness thereby. XX. F. He again levels the reproach of despising the divine ordinances. Whoso piously accepts the burden laid on him, finds it turn to his advantage. XXI. S. [not preserved] XXII. F. (What the sufferer has praised is not in fact to be ambitioned. Such advantages) quickly come to nothing. The rich scoundrel, who has attained wealth, finds his life exposed to the assassin. And what has the complainer gained by rejecting the divine will? He who submits has at least his daily bread.

XXIII. S. Observation of life shows the world to be full of contradictions. (It is evident that events are not controlled on any consistent principle. The lot of men depends on arbitrary decisions.) While a father labours in the canals, his firstborn son enjoys rest and comfort. Again the eldest brother lives proud as a lion; the younger has to be content with driving a mule. Or, on the contrary, the heir is driven to wandering round the streets and has to depend on his younger brother for the necessities of life. XXIV. F. The friend repeats:

[1] Strophes IX, X, and XI have not been found.

The thought of a god is as unfathomable as the inmost
heaven ;
His wisdom is weighty and beyond the reach of man.

(This is true. But there is consistency in the world.) The firstborn whether of man or beast is less well endowed than the second. (This is mysterious ; but) man cannot comprehend the decisions of the gods. XXV. S. (If virtue is indeed right and advantageous, why do men unite in acting as if it were not ?) They praise and help the powerful, regardless of their murders, wickedness, and lying ; they thrust aside the wretched and miserable, though they are honourable and have never caused harm. And such is his own experience. XXVI. F. (This time the friend admits the truth of what the sufferer has just said. Men do behave in a disgraceful way.) When the gods fashioned mankind, they endowed them with crafty and false speech. They flatter the rich ; they treat the unfortunate with contempt and injustice.

XXVII. The sufferer is given the last word. He begs for help. He has experienced neither help nor encouragement. His life has been quiet and humble. He prays that the god that rejected him, may now come to his help and that the angry goddess may take pity on him.

He thus silently admits that his rebellious attitude towards the gods was wrong ; that, though he cannot understand the reasons for the divine decisions, his duty is humbly to submit. The dialogue thus ends with the victory of virtue, but the problem remains unsolved. Man must be content with his own ignorance and put his trust in the unfathomable wisdom of the gods.[1]

* * *

Another text must not pass unnoticed which does not indeed speak of suffering but is connected with our subject

[1] Translations by B. Landsberger in *Zeitschrift für Assyriologie* 43 (1936) 32–76, by E. Ebeling in Gressmann, *Texte*, 287–91, by R. H. Pfeiffer in Pritchard, *Texts*, 438–40. P. Dhorme, ' Ecclésiaste ou Job ? ' in *Revue Biblique* 32 (1923) 1–27. This last publication was the first in which the dialogue form of the text was recognised.

in that it is generally understood to teach that there is no absolute standard of values in life and that, all said and done, death is to be preferred to life. This text is also in the form of a dialogue, this time between a master and his slave, and has been given the title of ' A Pessimistic Dialogue between a Master and his Slave '. That the subordinate is a slave and not merely a servant is shown by the master's final declaration that he intends to kill him. The text is not too well preserved and the translation not everywhere certain. In the cuneiform tablets the dialogue is divided into episodes or scenes by horizontal lines, though the position of these is not in all cases uniform in the different witnesses to the text. The division here followed is that of Ebeling. Except for the final episode the dialogue follows a rigid scheme. First the master announces his intention to undertake some course of action. The slave at once agrees and encourages his master by dwelling on the advantages of the proposal. The master then abruptly announces his intention of not undertaking the same enterprise, and the slave again, without any expression of surprise at the capriciousness of his master, at once agrees that the original proposal should not be carried out and proceeds to enumerate the advantages of abandoning it.

The first proposal is to visit the palace, the second to take a meal.

' Slave, do what I tell you ! ' ' Yes, master, yes ! '

' Bring me water for my hands straightaway and give it to me. I want a meal '.

' Have a meal, master, have a meal. Regular meals bring cheerfulness.

' Shamash [the sun god] comes to a meal eaten in cheerfulness and with clean hands '.

' No, slave, I will not take a meal.'

' Don't take a meal, master, don't take a meal !

' Hunger, then eating, thirst, then drinking, is the right course '. [1]

[1] This must be the meaning of the slave's remark, which literally translated runs : ' Hunger eating thirst drinking on a man comes '. As this is said in approval of the master's decision not to have a meal, it must express the

There follow proposals of the master to take the chariot to go hunting, to face his personal enemy, and to build a house. Then, with some probable restorations of a damaged text, comes the following :

'Slave, do what I tell you !' 'Yes, master, yes !'
'When my opponent at law speaks (?), I shall remain silent'.
'Remain silent, master, remain silent ; silence is better than speech'.
'No, slave, I will not remain silent when my opponent speaks (?)'.
'Do not remain silent, master, do not remain silent !
'If you do not open your mouth, your opponent will rejoice'.

The damaged text of the last line is of difficult interpretation. It might mean 'the other litigant will make petition against' or 'will be hostile to' ; but the end of the line is missing. The next two proposals deal with starting a rebellion and with falling in love with a woman. Again the considerations for and against are of a purely utilitarian and self-regarding order. The next decision is to offer a sacrifice and leads to astonishing reflections.

'Slave, do what I tell you !' 'Yes, master, yes !'
'Fetch me water for my hands straightaway ; give it me ; I'll offer a sacrifice to my god'.
'Offer it, master, offer it ! The man who offers a sacrifice to his god, has a glad heart !
'He wins return on return'.
'No, slave, I'll not make a sacrifice to my god'.
'Don't, master, don't offer a sacrifice !
'You'll teach the god to go after you like a dog,
'Whether he demands of you an act of cult or the omission of an inquiry or whatever it be'.

thought that it is wise not to do so when a man is neither hungry nor thirsty. The explanation given by Ebeling, Meissner, and Stamm that eating and drinking are natural necessities, which no one can escape, does not suit the context.

The next two exchanges deal with providing foodstuffs for the land and of doing something undefined but beneficial for it.

'Slave, listen to me!' 'Yes, master, yes!'
'Now I mean to do something beneficial for my country'.
'Do it, master, do it!
'The man who confers a benefit on his country
'—his good deed is placed in Marduk's urn'.
'No, slave, I will not do something beneficial for my country'.
'Don't do it, master, don't do it!
'Go up on to the ancient mounds and walk around them!
'See the skulls of more recent and of ancient men!
'Which is the evil-doer, which the benefactor?'

It is impossible to distinguish them. The final lot of all is the same. And the master is left to infer that it is consequently of no importance whether they did good in their lifetime or not. This brings the series of proposed actions and their rejections together with the respective advantages of each course to an end. The allusion to death in the last prepares the way for the final interchange.

'Slave, listen to me!' 'Yes, master, yes!'
'Now, what is good?
'To break my neck and your neck
'To throw (ourselves) into the river—that is good'.
'Who is so tall that he can reach up into heaven?
Who is so wide that he can embrace the earth?'

'No, slave, I will kill you and send you ahead of myself'.

'How indeed would my master survive me for three days?'[1]

[1] Transliterated text and translation by E. Ebeling in *Quellen zur Kenntnis der babylonischen Religion* (Leipzig 1919) 51–70 (=*Mitteilungen der Vorderasiatischen Gesellschaft* 23 [1918 : 2]). Translations by E. Ebeling in Gressmann, *Texte*, 284–7, and by R. H. Pfeiffer in Pritchard, *Texts*, 437f.; partial translations by G. B. Gray in *Expository Times* 31 (1920) 440–3 and B. Meissner, *Babylonien und Assyrien* 2 (Heidelberg 1925) 433f. See also H. Zimmern in *Zeitschrift für Assyriologie* 34 (1922) 87f. and Stamm, *Leiden*, 14–16

The identity of the speaker is not indicated in the original Babylonian tablets except by the sense, and there has been some difference of opinion as to the correct assignment in this last interchange between master and slave. Most allot the speeches as above. Ebeling, however, assigns lines 3 and 4 as well as 5 and 6 to the slave. Against this it may be urged that the slave would scarcely venture to suggest breaking his master's neck, that according to the analogy of the previous conversations lines 5 and 6 should be a comment of the slave's commending his master's proposal, that, again according to analogy, the master's words in line 7 are a reversal of a previous proposal of his own. The meaning of lines 5 and 6 does not lie on the surface for us. Stamm suggests that the slave conveys the thought that man is too insignificant a creature to comprehend the laws of the world. But this does not convey the expected complete approval of the master's pronouncement. His meaning is rather that man is too feeble and helpless to escape out of the world and thereby avoid the incidence of the universal law of mortality there reigning. That is to say, death must come and if the master decides that it must come now, well, nothing can be done about it. But the slave does not want to die. In his next comment he suggests the inconvenience that will result to his master from putting him to death, for how could he manage for even a few days without his accustomed services.

These considerations raise the question as to the real character of this intriguing text. All writers on the subject treat it as reflecting in all seriousness a pessimistic outlook on life. Yet Stamm speaks of the theme being developed in an 'almost playful fashion'; Zimmern comments on 'the somewhat burlesque tone' of the dialogue and the bad temper or ill-humour of the master; Meissner calls it 'quite burlesque'; and Gray speaks of 'the low irreverence' manifest in the dialogue about the proposal to offer a sacrifice. All these comments are justified, but they militate strongly against the idea that the composition was intended as a serious contribution on a serious theme with the considered teaching that there are no absolute values in life, and indeed that life is not worth living. This last suggestion is countered by the fact that the master does not intend to make away with himself and that the slave puts forward a reason why the master should not make an end of him.

The more natural interpretation of the piece understands it as a parody or jocose presentment of the obsequious slave. Whatever the master wants or does not want, the slave instantly approves of his decision and seeks for reasons in support of it. He does not stop to weigh the cogency or truth of his own words. In the end the master tires of it, pretends to take the slave seriously and at the face value of his own words, and puts him to the test. On the slave's own showing nothing is really good or really worthwhile in this world, and therefore, the master suggests, the best solution is for both of them to die. This suggestion he has no intention of carrying into effect, but, when the slave half-heartedly approves even of this, precisely because he is an obseqious slave, the master counters by declaring that he will not kill himself but only the slave who thinks or rather pretends to think such a course desirable. At this even the slave recoils and protests, but, because he is the slave he has been depicted, does so on the ground of his master's interest. This is the climax of the piece, by which the master unveils the unreality and insincerity of the slave's obsequious agreement and commendations.

Those who desire will find fuller references in the following: M. Jastrow, *The Religion of Babylonia and Assyria*, Boston 1898, and *Die Religion Babyloniens und Assyriens*, 2 vols., Giessen 1905, 1912 ; E. Dhorme, *La religion assyro-babylonienne* Paris 1910, and *Les religions de Babylonie et d'Assyrie*, Paris 1945 = *Mana, Introduction à l'Histoire des Religions*, I ; A. Condamin, 'La religion des Babyloniens et Assyriens' in Huby, *Christus*, 501–40, also *Babylonia and Assyria* in *Lectures* (CTS) ; H. Zimmern, 'Babylonians and Assyrians' in ERE II 309–19 ; A. Jeremias, 'Babylonian Ethics and Morality' in ERE V 444–7 ; Rowley, *Submission* (see its index).

Chapter III

THE FIRST SIN AND ITS CONSEQUENCES

As opposed to the Mazdaean doctrine of dualism the fundamental Hebrew belief was that there is one Creative Principle and one only. This is the burden of the first chapter of Genesis where God is described as working His will in the material creation by His mere word. It is true that before the creation of man God says 'Let us make man in our image and likeness', 1:26, but the text goes on to say 'And God created man in his image; in the image of God he created him', thus attributing the work of creation to God alone. And there is no doubt that in the mind of the sacred writer the previous use of the plural did not denote the association of other beings with God in the creative act. The expression is probably an example of the rare use of the plural of majesty. There is thus no question of the Hebrew theologians attributing the presence of evil in the world to an independent, eternal but malign power. The whole of the Old Testament cries out against the idea.

And all the works of this one Creator were good. This is stated explicitly four times in the Hebrew text, after the creative acts of the first, third, fourth, and fifth days. The Greek Septuagint text has the same remark also of the work of the second day, and its absence from the Hebrew will be due to a scribal error. Then after the crowning work of the creation of man on the sixth day both the Hebrew and the Greek unite in recording that 'God saw all that he had made, and lo! it was very good', 1:31. Thus all those systems were condemned in advance, which, like Manichaeism and Encratism, were to teach that parts of the created world are evil.

As all the material world was created good, so also was man. He came forth from the hand of his Creator innocent and happy. Not only was he innocent of sin, which clearly he could not yet have committed, but he was free from any internal impulse to sin, such as we call concupiscence. His lower nature was entirely subject to his higher faculties. The body was subject to the rule of reason. This is indicated in the text of the Bible not only by the statement that what God had made was good but also by the statement that Adam and Eve, though naked, 'were not ashamed', 2:25. That is to say, in spite of their nakedness they had no reason to feel ashamed. In their condition clothing was not in any way required. But the story does not end there. After their sin, then and then only they became conscious of their nakedness and of its unsuitability. Then they understood the necessity of garments and provided themselves with a modest loin-covering made of fig-leaves, 3:7. In this way the sacred writer describes how they passed on account of their sin into the condition common to later humanity, a condition from which they had been free when created by God.

Their innocence, of course, cannot be understood to mean that they were so simple as not to know the distinction between right and wrong. It is clear from the story that they did. The command given by God to abstain from certain food presupposes the knowledge that it would be wrong to disobey; and the sequel shows that Adam and Eve had this knowledge. It was a guilty conscience that prompted them to hide from God after eating the forbidden fuit, 3:8, and they would not have received the punishment in fact allotted to them, had they acted without the consciousness that they were acting sinfully.

That Adam was in full possession of the use of reason is further indicated by the incident of his naming the animals. God wished him to understand that he was alone and that something essential was lacking to him. Therefore, the text says, God brought to Adam all the beasts of the field and all the birds of the air to see what he would call them, 2:19. Several points must be noted about this simple statement. In the first place, nothing is said about all the animals of the whole world. The text is speaking of the Garden of Eden in which Adam had been placed by God, and the universal expressions are limited by that very fact to the brute creation that had its home with him in the Garden. Secondly, the text does not speak of any miraculous action of God in causing all the animals to come into Adam's presence, though, if we incautiously read the narrative with western eyes and western modes of thought, we may well fall into the error of so interpreting it. This is clear from the Hebrew habit of attributing everything directly to God, the prime cause, without mention of the action of creatures, the secondary causes. And this, properly understood, is not incorrect. As the philosophers express it, 'Qui facit per alium, facit per se'. This adage expresses the truth that he who gives to others the power and the authority or right to act, equivalently does himself what they do. This second chapter of Genesis presents an excellent example in the statement that 'God had not rained upon the earth', 2:5. It was God who created the physical causes of rain and gave them the laws of their nature, so that if no rain had yet fallen, it could correctly be said that God had not yet caused it to rain or God had not yet rained. Hence the words 'God brought the animals to Adam' do not say more than that in the ordinary course of things Adam came to see the various species of animals that lived in the Garden, for it is not said or implied that all the animals came into his presence at one and the same time. How long it took Adam to become acquainted with them all did not interest the narrator and he is silent on the point. In the third place must be noticed the purpose of Adam's naming of the animals. To understand this we must bear in mind the meaning or function of names among the Hebrews. For us, at least in general, names are mere labels, necessary to distinguish one thing or person from another. Not so for the Hebrews. In their minds names were conceived as manifesting the nature, function, or office of the person or thing named. Hence the change of names, such as Abram to Abraham, of Sarai to Sarah, of Jacob to Israel. It should be added, however, that in the case of persons the further element may enter that the change of name sometimes has the purpose of manifesting the authority and power of him who imposes the new name. This seems to have been the object in view when Pharaoh Nechao altered the name of Eliakim to Jehoiakim on the occasion of his nomination to the throne of Judah, 2 (4), Kg 22:34, and when Nabuchodonosor changed the name of Mattaniah to Zedekiah on his appointment as sovereign in that land, 2 (4), Kg 24:17. This being the function of names, then, to manifest the nature, function, or office of the object named, the ability to impose suitable names supposes a corresponding degree of knowledge in the person naming. Therefore, if Adam was competent to impose names, he possessed already at least knowledge adequate for the task. The purpose of his naming the animals does not directly concern us here, but, briefly stated, was that he might acquire sufficient acquaintance with the animal creation of the Garden to realise that among them all he was nevertheless alone. No one of them was suitable to be his consort and helpmeet. When he had come to understand this, then God presented him with Eve as his wife.

Such, then, was the innocence of our first parents, freedom from sin and freedom from any internal allurement to sin, but coupled with the use of reason by which they knew how to distinguish good from evil. And this moral innocence was matched by the felicity of the material conditions of their existence which were unmarred by physical ills. This is manifested by the fact that God did not intend them to die. They were mortal by nature, but had the privilege of immortality in the sense that they would not have died, had they been faithful to the service of their Creator. In forbidding the use of the Tree of Knowledge of Good and Evil, God warned Adam of the disastrous consequences of disobedience: 'In the day that thou dost eat thereof', that is, according to the Hebrew idiom 'whensoever thou dost eat thereof', 'dying thou shalt die', 2:17. The words do not mean, as the sequel shows, that death would visit the offence on the day of transgression, but that the gift of immortality would be lost by the transgressor who would become subject to the natural consequences of possessing a perishable human body. This divine threat was confirmed by God after the sin by the words 'Dust thou art and to dust thou shalt return', 3:19.

These two privileges of immortality and the absence of the need of clothing as protection against cold are an indication of the happy conditions of life enjoyed in the Garden of Eden. For these privileges carry with them immunity from the ordinary dangers of life which all subsequent generations of mankind have experienced. The Book of Genesis thus puts before its readers the picture of an innocent, happy life, free from all cares and anxieties, and in the fatherly purpose of God destined so to remain.

Now the sacred writer's purpose is to explain how mankind came to be in the sad state in which we actually find ourselves. He has shown that it was not God's intention that man should be subject to the miseries of 'this vale of tears'. What then brought the change about? It was no capricious act on God's part, no arbitrary change of His design; neither was it due to any working of inexorable laws of fate, a conception dear to the Stoics but unknown to the Hebrews. For them God was supreme, the Ruler of the universe, Himself subject to no power whatsoever. He might have created man as a rational creature with full knowledge of his actions but without the power of himself deciding what those actions should be. Such a man would have served God and done God's will just as God's will is done by inanimate nature and by the brute creation, for he would have had no power except to follow the law of his nature. His life would have been good, but only for the reason that he could not make it otherwise, and such a good life would have been no credit to man and he could have acquired no merit thereby. Moreover, man, if so constituted, would have been deprived of his highest possible attainment. He would in his measure have presented vestiges of the divine perfections just as do all inanimate creatures by the very fact of their being the thought and design of God produced in material form. But he would not have had the possibility of reflecting the divine goodness by the voluntary practice of virtue. And that is the highest perfection which man can attain, to make himself, his own free choice helped by divine grace, an image of God not merely in the physical order but in the moral sphere by the striving for and the eventual attainment of real holiness. And this is the high dignity which God Almighty designed for man and for this purpose He endowed man with free will. Man was to have the free choice of serving God or of refusing that service, of accepting that service in a higher or in a lower degree.

Adam and Eve, therefore, had to make their own choice. The service of God was not to be thrust on them. Constituted as they were with no internal allurement to sin and situated in the Garden of Eden where also external attraction to sin was absent, they seemed exposed to no temptation. What the precise nature of their sin was, has probably not been revealed to us. The figurative language, so characteristic of the Old Testament, makes it most probable that the eating of the fruit of the Tree of Knowledge is symbolical only. Even, however, if this element of the story is understood literally, there is nothing unjust in the prohibition and the severe penalty attached to disobedience. On the contrary, one precept only was imposed on Adam and Eve, and that one easy of observance, as a test of their willingness to submit to their condition as creatures of God, singularly blessed and privileged by Him as they were. The name of the tree, being that of the knowledge of good and of evil, may be understood from the story. By their obedience or disobedience our first parents were to show whether they were prepared to follow the good or to choose the evil. If they chose the good, they would continue to enjoy the good existence which was theirs. If they chose to do evil, they would learn what physical and material evil is. And the only knowledge mentioned as accruing to them as a result of their sin is the realisation that they were naked. They now had knowledge of the difference between their fallen state and the state of complete innocence they had previously been given. But when the power of evil lurking in the serpent, or rather symbolised by the serpent, came to tempt Eve, it made use of a meaning at least suggested by the name. This name, that of the knowledge of good and of evil, is composed of two contrary elements, namely, good and evil, and it is a common Hebrew idiom to denote totality by the conjunction of the two opposites, just as we speak in English of destroying something 'root and branch' to denote complete and utter destruction. Indeed this common phrase is itself probably of biblical origin derived from the text of Malachy 4:1, where we read in the Authorised Version 'it shall leave them neither root nor branch' (wording found previously in the Bishop's Bible and retained in the Revised Version). The phrase, therefore, 'the knowledge of good and of evil', at least suggests the knowledge of all things or omniscience. This idea was subtly used by the serpent when it suggested that God was withholding a great benefit from them and that if they ate the forbidden fruit, they would 'be as God knowing good and evil', that is they would acquire the prerogative of omniscience, 3:5. Their sin is thus represented as a sin of disobedience rooted in pride and accompanied by a credulous adherence to a most unworthy insinuation against their divine benefactor.

It should perhaps be added that attempts have been made both in ancient and modern times to determine more accurately the specific nature of the sin. But no such effort has met with success. It could not have been a sin of gluttony. The sternest moralist would not find a sin of gluttony in the consumption of a fruit; and for all the text tells us, the temptation very likely came, as certainly it would be likely to come, at a time when the need of sustenance called for a repast. Neither is there any probability in the suggestion that in some obscure way the sin was connected with the worship or at least recognition of false divinities. The story has no reference to polytheism and it is a problem how such an idea could have entered the head of Adam or Eve. They knew the one true God and knew that He had created them and placed them in the Garden of Eden. There was nothing to suggest the possibility of other divinities. A third proposal is that the sin was in some way sexual. It is true that sex appears with some prominence in the story but not in connection with the temptation or sin; and the statement of the serpent that disregard of the divine prohibition would in some way make them like to God does not lend itself to this interpretation. The allusions to sex are amply accounted for without any connection with the sin committed, for the story explains the condition in which mankind actually finds itself and, in this, sexual relations necessarily play a very important part, being concerned with the preservation of the species. The other fundamental instinct of the human race is for the preservation of the individual ; and, as the prime need to be met in order to satisfy this instinct is that of food, the mention of food is also prominent in the story of the Garden of Eden. The allusions both to sex and to food were inevitable in the account of the creation and Fall, and neither lends any support to an interpretation of the specific character of the sin committed. St Augustine pours scorn on the thought that the sin could have consisted in the premature use of marriage. God had made male and female, and it was His will that the race should multiply.[1]

After the sin followed the judicial sentence on the culprits. This in general was equivalent to the withdrawal of the extraordinary privileges that had been theirs. They were already conscious even before the sentence of having lost a precious gift. This consciousness was involved in their new realisation of the need of clothing, as mentioned above, p. 44. God tells them now that they have lost the gift of immortality, for they must return to dust. In this way the hagiographer explains the origin of the present condition of mankind. Firstly, men are subject to concupiscence, to the rebellion of their lower nature against reason, a condition of our nature later to be referred to by St Paul. ' The flesh ', he says, ' lusteth against the spirit and the spirit against the flesh ; for these are contrary to one another ', Gal 5:17, and again, ' I find then a law that when I have a will to do good, evil is present with me ', Rom 7:21. Man is conscious of this lack of harmony in his nature and does not feel in himself that absolute mastery that he would desire. But he can and often does conquer the lower desires that meet with his reprobation. And the very fact of this internal struggle convinces him that

[1] *De Genesi ad litteram* XI 41 (Migne, P.L. 34:452 ; CSEL XXVIII 376)

he is composed not merely of the flesh and bones he can touch and count. Flesh and blood do not struggle against flesh and blood. There is no such struggle in the animals. They follow without demur the promptings of their animal nature. If there is a struggle, as there is in man, a struggle in which flesh and blood is one of the combatants, then that against which it struggles is not flesh and blood, but something of a different and a higher order. And that something of a different and higher order is what is named spirit or soul. Man is a composite being, made up out of heterogeneous elements, of flesh and spirit, body and soul. The second condition of our existence that weighs heavily on man is our subjection to the inexorable dominion of death. The origin of this too is explained by the story of the Fall. So strongly do men in general cling to life and so abhorrent is the idea of the complete cessation of being that in this very longing for existence pagan philosophers found an argument for immortality.

These then are the two main features of our lives of which Genesis describes the origin. Besides, specially mentioned in the divine sentence of condemnation, are the pains of childbirth and the subjection of womanhood which has been so prevalent in the past and in various parts of the world. And in spite of this subjection there is in woman a natural leaning on man, a natural desire to be joined in union with him. 'Thy longing shall be to thy husband, but he shall have dominion over thee', 3:16. Then again, the normal lot of man is the necessity of hard and continual work to support himself and his family. This too is mentioned in God's verdict: 'Cursed is the earth in thy work; with labour and toil shalt thou eat thereof all the days of thy life', 3:17; and further, 'in the sweat of thy brow shalt thou eat bread till thou return to the earth out of which thou wast taken', 3:19.

The origin of all the hardship and misery of the world is explained in Genesis. None of it was in God's original plan. Its presence and prevalence are the fruit of sin. This is the Old Testament teaching. Thus the sin of Adam entailed consequences not for himself alone but also for his posterity; and this involves considerations which must be reserved for our next chapter.

Before, however, passing on to these considerations, we must comment on the unique character of this biblical story of Paradise and the Fall of Man. Nothing to be compared to it has been found in the literature of the ancient Near East. There is nothing like it in the innumerable Sumerian, Babylonian, and Assyrian tablets now known. S. Langdon published a book in 1915 to which he gave the title *A Sumerian Epic of Paradise, the Flood, and the Fall of Man*, of which a French translation appeared in 1919. Knowledge of the difficult Sumerian language was, however, at that time still in its initial stages, and scholars have since recognised that the poem in question says nothing of any of the subjects named in Langdon's title.[1] Many more tablets undoubtedly remain to be unearthed in the soil of Mesopotamia, and the question arises whether it is likely that such a story did exist and may therefore yet be found. H. Zimmern seems to have thought it probable, for he wrote: 'As yet at least we cannot prove the existence in Babylon of a so-called Paradise legend proper'.[2] And Alfred Jeremias wrote: 'Should the excavations some day bring to light a Babylonian narrative of the Fall, it would be no matter for surprise'.[3] But this anticipation is subject to important reservations.

According to Babylonian ideas mankind was created mortal; immortality was reserved by the gods to themselves. In the *Epic of Gilgamesh* the following address is made to the hero of the poem:

> O Gilgamesh, why dost thou haste from place to place?
> The life thou seekest, thou shalt not find.
> When the gods created man,
> They established death for man;
> They kept life in their own hands.

The address goes on as a corollary to encourage Gilgamesh to enjoy life while he may.[4]

[1] See VDBS I 739f. [2] ERE II 314*ab* [3] ERE V 446*a*
[4] Dhorme, *Choix*, 301; Thompson, *Epic*, 46; Contenau, *L'Épopée*, 131

In the *Myth of Adapa* it is related how Adapa, who was a son of the god Ea, lost the opportunity of gaining immortality. Anu, the great god of heaven, offered him 'food of life' and 'water of life', but he declined the proffered gifts thinking them to be 'food of death' and 'water of death', which Ea had previously warned him to refuse. The purpose of the myth is not to explain, as H. Zimmern suggests, why man is mortal, but rather to teach the impossibility of the acquisition of immortality by man.[1] The same lesson is taught by the theft from Gilgamesh of the plant of life he had been told of in his wanderings by Uta-napishtim, the hero of the Babylonian Flood. This plant was named 'The old turned young' designating its powers of rejuvenation. But Gilgamesh was destined not to eat of it, and while he was enjoying a bathe, a serpent maliciously stole it from him.[2]

Then there is good ground for thinking that the Babylonians had no conception of the reality underlying the words of Genesis 'The eyes of them both were opened and they knew that they were naked', 3:7. The Babylonians seem to have been too licentious for such a doctrine. This is the description given by A. Jeremias: 'Drunkenness and debauchery, lust and sensuality, seem to have been very prevalent among the men. And as the people, so the gods. The pictures of carousing deities in the Creation epic—of deities who drink till they fall under the table—reflect the customs of the day. The licentious cult of Ishtar, the representations of sexual life in the Gilgamesh epic and in Ishtar's descent into the underworld, as also the fact that the place of sexual intercourse was the public street, all point to conditions of gross sensuality'. [3]

A further ground for doubt about the existence of any story of the Fall among the Babylonians is provided by the purpose for which man was conceived to have been created according to the sixth tablet of *Enuma elish*, the epic of creation. This has been well explained by R. Labat. The

[1] H. Zimmern, ERE II 314*b*; J. Plessis, VDBS I 740–2; Dhorme, *Choix*, 148–61

[2] Dhorme, *Choix*, 312f.; Thompson, *Epic*, 55f.; Contenau, *L'Épopée*, 148f.

[3] ERE V 447*a*

guilt of having incited Tiamat and her followers to make war on the gods was fixed on Kingu. This god was therefore chained and slain and of his blood Ea created the human race, imposing on man the task of freeing the gods by taking their guilt on himself. The guilt of the gods is first laid on Kingu, who was one of their number, by a process of substitution. He in turn by the use made of his blood passed the guilt to human kind, in whose mortal frames the chastisement is perpetuated. The young gods had incurred guilt by killing Apsu and Mummu and thus introducing death into the universe. By the fact that the human race is in part formed of divine blood it has a link with the gods which rendered it possible to transfer their guilt to men. And the service of the gods for which man was created thus consists in freeing the gods by bearing the guilt in their place.[1]

Other statements about the purpose of man's creation are not necessarily in conflict with this. Thus in the *Chaldaean Cosmogony*, 19–20, it is said: 'To enable the gods to dwell in a habitation pleasant to the heart (Marduk) created mankind'.[2] It is not quite clear whether the purpose named should be joined as in the above translation or with the preceding formation of solid land where previously there had been only a watery mass. But even if this was the writer's intention, it would remain true that mankind not only built the temples but was necessary as an instrument for the work. But this is not to be taken as a complete statement of the purpose intended for man and does not in any way contradict the idea set forth in *Enuma elish*. Neither statement is presented as part of a comprehensive theological disquisition and each author stresses the element congenial to his theme. This is quite in accord with the way biblical writers give partial accounts of the doctrine they have in mind, each in the interest of the particular point of view that concerned him at the time. This fact is illustrated by another passage in which in addition to work on temples, man's task is said to be labour on the land to

[1] R. Labat, *Le poème babylonien de la Création* (Paris 1935) 1483*n.*, on Tablet VI lines 1–38

[2] Dhorme, *Choix*, 87

render it fertile.[1] Finally, the wide diffusion of the Creation epic must have ensured general knowledge and acceptance of its doctrine.

Thus, according to our sources, man was created mortal and almost certainly subject to the sway of human passion. He was also created of a guilty element. These considerations render it impossible that the Babylonians can have had a story of the Fall in any way resembling the story of Genesis.

[1] Quoted by J. Plessis in VDBS I 727

Chapter IV

CORPORATE SOLIDARITY

Corporate solidarity is a fact of human experience with which all of us have been familiar even from our earliest years. It entered into our conscious lives from the time that we became aware of belonging to one definite family as distinct from all others. It was a fact present in our daily experience though without reflection or speculation about it, and the words 'corporate solidarity' would have conveyed nothing to our minds at that age even if we had heard them. Later than the realisation of our membership of a unit which we call a 'family' came the further knowledge that our family together with many similar units constituted a vastly larger unit, which we call a 'nation'. And with this knowledge came also that of the existence of other similar units or nations. Our devotion, loyalty, and affection for our family became enriched by a sentiment of satisfaction in our membership of the larger unit and by a sentiment of loyalty and affection which we name 'patriotism'.

The growth of this knowledge and these loyalties was entirely due to outside influences and without any conscious reflection. Only with the development of reason and of our powers of intellect did we begin to understand how much we as individual human beings owed to our membership of these units. Not only external traits such as our dress, our manners, our speech, but our very thoughts and standards of value are due to the all-permeating influence of these units, the family and the nation. There are other intermediate units, such as the city and the county, which in greater or lesser measure attract our loyalty and influence our thoughts, outlook, and character, but for simplicity attention may be concentrated on the smallest and the largest, the family and the nation, which produce the most marked and the most enduring effects on our characters. Everyone is a child of his age. No one would be what he is, had he been born in another age. Still less would anyone be what he is, had he come into the world at another time and as a member of another nation. Not only would his speech have been different, his likes and dislikes, his manners, his very thoughts would have been quite other. All this shows how profound is the debt of every human being to his membership of the two great units, or, in other words, to the nature of the corporate personalities to which he actually belongs. There are, of course, men of outstanding gifts and independent minds, who give birth to new ideas and lead their contemporaries intellectually, socially, or in other ways. But even these men, who seem least under the influence of their environment, would not and could not have made the same inventions or had the same thoughts had they lived in other times and places, for even the most talented and outstanding men are conditioned by the inherited knowledge and culture of previous ages. No man is exempt from the working of this law that all human beings are children of their time and their environment. If we can conceive a person entirely uninfluenced by his own or previous generations, without any share of the knowledge accumulated by the efforts of the past or the present, that man would not even have a language with which to communicate with his fellow-men. So much to illustrate the profound influence exercised upon each and all of us by our membership of these units, by our corporate solidarity with them.

The consequences of this family and national solidarity as sanctioned by custom and law have varied in different races and at different stages of their development. In the ancient Near East the appreciation of this solidarity was remarkably strong and led to results surprising and even shocking to us. This may be illustrated from the records of various ancient peoples. A decree of the Egyptian monarch Nubu-kheper-Ra of the XVIIth dynasty proclaiming the punishment of a certain official named Teta for some traitorous act includes also his posterity : 'Let him be cast out upon the ground from the temple of my father Min ; let him be driven from his office in the temple, to the son of his son and the heir of his heir; may they be cast abroad upon the ground'.[1] The legal solidarity of the family was strong also in Babylonia. A case is recorded in which a woman named Belilit brought an action to recover a certain sum of money. This, it was proved, had been duly paid to her two sons, who had wrongfully put it to their own uses. The verdict of the court was that Belilit, instead of recovering the money she claimed, was mulcted in the same amount.[2] Examples may also be cited from the great legal code of Hammurabi, 1728–1686. § 116 enacts that if the surety for a debt should die in the house of the creditor as a result of ill-treatment, and the surety in question should be the son of the debtor, then the son of the creditor is to be executed. §§ 209 and 210 lay it down that if as a result of a blow struck at a (free) woman she should be deprived of her offspring, the offender is to be fined 10 shekels; but if the woman should herself die as a consequence, then the daughter of the offender is to be put to death. Similar laws are found in §§ 229 and 230. According to the former, if a house collapses and kills the owner on account of the negligence of the builder in not making the house secure, then the builder is to be put to death. But according to the following law, if as a result of this negligence and the ensuing disaster, the son of the owner loses his life, then the son of the builder is to be executed.[3] These laws rest on the solidarity of the family and on the principle of the *Lex Talionis*. This principle aimed at ensuring that the punishment should fit the crime as far as possible and that the penalty inflicted on the family of the offender should exactly correspond to the loss suffered by the injured family. In other words, the law considered not the person of the offender but his family. This is alien to our ideas, but at the time these laws were enacted and enforced, they awakened no sense of injustice. On the contrary, they had their root in the social conscience of the people

[1] W. M. Flinders Petrie, *A History of Egypt* I (London 1895) 136; H. R. Hall, *The Ancient History of the Near East* (London 1950[11]) 220f.

[2] ERE IX 479*a*

[3] J. Kohler and F. E. Peiser, *Hammurabi's Gesetz* I (Leipzig 1904)

and corresponded to the ideas of justice prevalent at the time. Given the solidary liability of the family, it is clear that there is nothing unjust in these laws. They are merely applications of that liability. The question of justice concerns this liability. And although it is difficult for us to think ourselves back into the mentality that considered the family to have solidary liability, it may well be that in certain societies and in certain stages of their social development the ends of justice were best served by this conception and its application in law. In our own days British justice in its relations with Arab tribes has found itself constrained to follow the principle of tribal solidarity and consequently of tribal responsibility in dealing with crimes committed by members of a tribe.

Similar conceptions were entertained among the Assyrians and the Hittites and similar applications were made in their laws. According to the code of the Assyrians if a man has used violence and dishonoured the virgin daughter of another man, the father of the injured daughter is entitled to have a similar dishonour inflicted on the wife of the ravisher.[1] In the extant record of a case of murder the murderer is to deliver his wife, brother, or son to the representative of his victim.[2] According to a Hittite law if anyone contests the justice of the king, his whole household is to be put to death.[3] This law dates from about the middle of the fourteenth century B.C. Some indication of Persian practice is given in the Bible. There it is narrated that King Darius ordered Daniel's accusers to be cast into the lions' den, they themselves together with their children and their wives.[4] The ten sons of Aman were slain by the Jews and Esther requested the king that their bodies should be hanged on the gibbet, a request which the king granted.[5] The story in Herodotus may also be recalled in which he relates that Darius put to death with Intaphernes all his children and relatives except his wife, her brother and

[1] G. R. Driver and J. C. Miles, *The Assyrian Laws* (Oxford 1935) 423
[2] *Ibid.*, p. 35
[3] F. Hrozny, *Code Hittite* (Paris 1922) p. 133 § 173
[4] Dan 6:24 (Aramaic text 25) [5] Esther 9:13f.

eldest son, whom her entreaties induced him to spare.[1] Into our own days this sentiment of family and tribal solidarity persists strongly among the Arabs. Terrible vengeance may be taken for a murder, but the whole proceedings are strictly controlled by tribal custom. Within the first three days not only the murderer but also his relatives may be massacred, his animals, his dwelling, and other property destroyed. But nothing of the murderer's property may be appropriated. It must be destroyed or left. After the three days the murderer, if he still survives, remains exposed to the vengeance of the next-of-kin of the murdered man. According to the law of blood revenge he must himself pay the penalty if this is possible. If he escapes beyond the reach of vengeance, then his father may be attacked or his son, or one of his relatives. Alien as these practices are to the sense of justice of civilised, sedentary societies, Père Jaussen, an experienced observer, has put it on record that in his opinion without this law of vengeance life in the desert would be impossible. 'As long as the desert remains the desert', he writes, 'blood vengeance, regulated by custom, will survive, and, we may say, will remain a necessity'.[2] In forming a judgment of these usages it is important that such considerations be borne in mind.

With these conceptions prevalent in the ancient and modern Near East in mind we shall be able to form a juster and more balanced view of ways of thought and action current in ancient Israel. There too the sense of family and national solidarity was very strong. Father and mother are to be treated with honour [3] and with respect.[4] Sons are to be attentive to their instructions and teaching,[5] and to their commands,[6] and hard things are said of unfilial conduct.[7] The son guilty of striking [8] or cursing [9] either of his parents is to be put to death. The bestowal of his daughters in marriage

[1] Herod. iii 119

[2] A. Jaussen, O. P., *Coutumes des Arabes au pays de Moab* (Paris 1908; Études Bibliques) 220–3

[3] Ex 20:12; Dt 5:16

[4] Lev 19:3

[5] Prov 1:8

[6] Prov 6:20

[7] Prov 19:26; 20:20; 28:24. Such conduct was not unknown, Ez 22:7, Mic 7:6; Prov 30:11, 17

[8] Ex 21:15

[9] Ex 21:17; Lev 20:9

was in the hands of the father [1] as it was his right also to procure a wife for his son,[2] though, in the nature of things, the mother would also make her voice heard.[3] The father had the right to sell his daughter as a bond-maid, a status which carried with it that of a concubine or secondary wife, if her master so desired.[4] The story of Jacob shows that the children of such secondary wives could have the same rights as those of the principal wife or wives. The story shows no distinction in the status of his twelve sons, though two of the mothers, Lia and Rachel, were wives of equal position, whereas the other two, Zelpha (Zilpah) and Bala (Bilhah) were handmaids or maid-servants.[5] This practice was derived from Babylonia whence Abraham came to Canaan. In the Code of Hammurabi it is laid down that a father could give or withhold full recognition to the sons of his handmaid according as he wished. If he gave them recognition by calling them 'my children', then they had equal rights with the children of his principal wife except that the chief heir was always to be a son of the latter.[6] Should the father withhold this recognition, then the children of his secondary wife were excluded from the inheritance.[7] The Israelite father could not, however, sell son or daughter into perpetual slavery. If Israelites wanted to be absolute owners of men or women, in other words to have them as true slaves without limit of time, they were obliged by law to procure them from foreigners.[8] Neither was it lawful for a man to prostitute his daughter.[9] The children could be taken in satisfaction of their parents' debts. It was in favour of a widow threatened with the loss of her two sons that Eliseus (Elisha) worked the miracle of the multiplication of oil.[10] This was in the ninth century B.C., and in the fifth

[1] Gen 29:19, 27
[2] Gen 24:4 ; 28:1f.
[3] Gen 27:46
[4] Ex 21:7–11
[5] Gen 29:23, 24, 28, 29
[6] Code of Hammurabi §170
[7] *Ibid.*, §171. A contract by which Shamash-nuri, the daughter of Ibi-Sha'an, was sold to be the secondary wife of Bununi-abi and the slave of Belissunu, his first wife, say be seen in J. Kohler and A. Ungnad, *Hammurabi's Gesetz* III (Leipzig 1909) 116 no. 424. The contract was drawn up in the presence of seven witnesses. To the name of each is added that of his father.
[8] Lev 25:44–46
[9] Lev 19:29
[10] 2(4) Kg 4:1

century we read in the Book of Nehemias that some fathers were obliged by poverty and debt to submit to the loss of their children.[1]

In patriarchal times at least, the father of a family could have his daughter-in-law burnt alive for unchastity, as is shown by the story of Judah and Thamar (Tamar).[2] And a ne'er-do-well and drunkard son could be stoned to death but only with the approbation of the elders of the city after the case had been heard at the gate which was the place of public meeting.[3] The Canaanites, who were conquered by the Israelites, practised abominable inhuman rites with which they sacrificed their children to their gods. The Israelites were warned on no account to sin in imitation of them. 'When Yahweh thy God shall have destroyed before thy face the nations, which thou goest in to dispossess, and when thou shalt have dispossessed them and dwelt in their land, beware lest thou be enticed after them after they are destroyed before thee, and lest thou seek after their gods, saying: As these nations have worshipped their gods, so also will I do. Thou shalt not do in like manner to Yahweh thy God, for they have done to their gods every abomination which Yahweh abhorreth even burning with fire their sons and their daughters to their gods'.[4] In spite of this and other warnings the Hebrews did adopt this savage cult as is testified by numerous passages of Scripture from the time of Achaz in the eighth century down to the destruction of Jerusalem and the fall of the Southern Kingdom early in the sixth. It was practised by King Achaz of Judah himself (736/5–727)[5]; it was practised in the Northern Kingdom[6]; and it was practised by King Manasses (698/7–643/2).[7] The good King Josias did his utmost to extirpate

[1] Neh 5:5, cp. Mt 18:25, where in the parable the creditor king ordered the debtor to be 'sold and his wife and children and all that he had and payment to be made'.

[2] Gen 38:24. In the Mosaic law this penalty is prescribed only for the daughter of a priest who profanes her father by playing the harlot, Lev 21:9. In the case of other women the penalty was stoning, Dt 22:21.

[3] Dt 21:18–21

[4] Dt 12:29–31; cp. Lev 18:21; 20:2–5; Dt 18:9–10; Wis 12:5

[5] 2(4) Kg 18:3; 2 Par 28:3

[6] 2(4) Kg 17:17

[7] 2(4) Kg 21:6; 2 Par 33:6

this abomination. To this end he defiled Topheth in Ge-Hinnom, the valley to the south of Jerusalem, where these sacrifices were offered.[1] That they were thus offered publicly in the close vicinity of Jerusalem we have also the repeated testimony of Jeremias.[2] Ezechiel indicates that the children sacrificed were the firstborn.[3] These sacrifices were strictly forbidden by the law, and consequently do not prove any legal right in the father to dispose of the lives of his offspring. Yet the publicity of the practice and its wide use, as indicated by the number of the references made to it, show that custom at least acknowledged such a right in the father, though the practice was almost certainly confined to infants. In the lawless days of the Judges when there was no king in Israel,[4] this *patria potestas* seems to have been absolute and to have extended to all members of the family, for Jephte (Jephthah) vowed to offer in sacrifice whoever should first come forth from his house to greet him on his return from the campaign against the Ammonites.[5] The same right seems to have been recognised in patriarchal times, when there was no authority higher than that of the father of the household. The right was never exercised, and the sacrifice of Isaac was not consummated. It was ordered by God to test Abraham's faith and obedience, but the fact of the divine command being given is itself an indication that custom recognised the existence of such a right in the father. In addition to the proof of the patriarch's virtue the purpose of the order seems to have been to demonstrate that the rights of Yahweh, the true God, were in no way inferior to those admitted by the pagan Canaanites in their gods, with this important difference that He would never exact the fulfilment of such a sacrifice.[6]

On account of the solidarity of the family and its members forming a closely knit unit they share alike in the blessings

[1] 2(4) Kg 23:10. On Ge-Hinnom as the prototype of the New Testament Gehenna see Sutcliffe, *Future Life*, 175f.

[2] Jer 7:31 ; 19:5–6 ; 32:35

[3] Ez 20:26 ; other references Ez 16:20–21 ; 20:31 ; 23:37 ; Ps 105(106): 37f.

[4] Jg 17:6 ; 21:24 (HT 25) ; 18:1

[5] Jg 11:31, 34–40

[6] Gen 22:1–18

and in the punishments merited by the head of the family. Thus it is said of Noe alone that he was just and perfect in his generation, for 'all flesh had corrupted its way upon the earth', yet his family was saved with him.[1] A striking instance of this solidarity with a holy ancestor is found in the concluding words of God's great promise to Isaac. God promised that He would multiply his seed like the stars of heaven and that in his seed all the nations of the earth should be blessed, 'because Abraham obeyed my voice and kept my precepts and commandments'.[2] Thus future generations are to be blessed because of their solidarity with the great patriarch whose life was so well-pleasing to God. In the same way God showed His mercy towards the kingdom of Judah and Jerusalem because of His servant David. Joram, king of Judah, did evil in the sight of God imitating the iniquities of the Northern Kingdom under the influence of his wife, Athalia, the daughter of Achab, king of Israel, and his pagan wife, Jezabel, who was a worshipper of Baal. Yet 'Yahweh was not willing to destroy Judah for David his servant's sake, as he had promised to give him a lamp and to his children always'.[3] So also when Sennacherib, the king of Assyria, was besieging Jerusalem in the reign of Ezechias, God routed the powerful invading army for the sake of David: 'I will protect this city and will save it for my own sake and for David my servant's sake'.[4] Obededom gave shelter to the Ark in his own dwelling and this brought a blessing not only on Obededom himself but also on his whole household: 'It was told king David that Yahweh had blessed Obededom and all that were his because of the ark of God'.[5] The general principle is found enunciated in various passages of the Psalms and the Book of Proverbs.

> The just man walks in his innocence;
> Blessed are his children after him.[6]

[1] Gen 6:9, 12 [2] Gen 26:2–5
[3] 2(4) Kg 8:18f.
[4] 2(4) Kg 19:34. See also 1(3) Kg 11:12, 32; 15:4 f.
[5] 2 Sam 6:11f.
[6] Prov 20:7. See also 11:21; 14:26

In the following passage, as is shown by the parallelism, both the 'seed' and the 'upright generation' are the posterity of the religious-minded man.

> Blessed is the man with reverence for Yahweh,
> Who delights greatly in his commands.
> Mighty in the land shall be his seed ;
> An upright generation shall be blessed.[1]

The possession of the land promised to the seed of the just in another text is an allusion to the divine promise made to Abraham and to Israel after him that they should possess the land of Canaan.[2]

> Who is the man with reverence for Yahweh,
> Whom he teaches of the way he should choose ?
> His soul abides in prosperity,
> And his seed shall possess the land.[3]

As with the merits, so also with the demerits of the father of the family. By reason of the solidarity of the family his penalty may fall on his children and posterity. David had given occasion to the enemies of the Lord to blaspheme by his sin with the wife of Urias the Hittite and in punishment the child thus born to him was to be lost to him by death.[4] Similarly when the son of the widow of Sarephta died, the good woman thought it must be on account of some iniquity of her own.[5] When Saul judged Achimelech to be guilty of high treason, he condemned him to death and all his father's house.[6] In Deuteronomy it is said that if any man fell into idolatry, the Lord would blot out his name from under heaven.[7] And the blotting out of a man's name meant the extinction of his family so that there would be no one of his posterity left to preserve the memory of it. On account of the judicial murder of Naboth, the robbery of his vineyard, and Achab's other

[1] Ps 111(112):1f.
[2] Gen 15:7 ; Ex 20:12 ; Dt 4:1
[3] Ps 24(25):12f. See also Pss 36(37):25 ; 101(102):29
[4] 2 Sam 12:14
[5] 1(3) Kg 17:18
[6] 1 Sam 22:18
[7] Dt 29:20 (HT 19)

iniquities he was threatened with the destruction of his family, but when he humbled himself before God and did penance, the evil was postponed to his son's days.[1] And it is related in the annals of Jehu that he slew Joram, the son of Achab, and procured the death of all his family.[2] As a result of their rebellion Core, Dathan, and Abiron perished with their wives and children.[3] According to the common understanding of the text Achan, who had transgressed by stealing gold and silver from Jericho already consecrated to God, was put to death together with his sons and daughters.[4] As A. Fernandez remarks on this incident, their common fate, considered in the light of history, was due to the solidarity of the family rather than to any share in the theft of the valuables. The same strong sense of solidarity is the explanation also of David's act in handing over to the Gibeonites two sons and five grandsons of Saul's to satisfy their desire of revenge for that king's slaughter of men of their race contrary to the oath sworn to them by Josue and the leading men of the Israelites. The long, devoted vigil of Respha by the crucified corpses of her five sons has made her a model of maternal affection.[5] Finally in this connection may be quoted the sentence pronounced with divine authority by Jeremias in the sixth century against Semaias: 'Behold, I will punish Semaias the Nehelamite and his seed. He shall not have a man to dwell in the midst of this people and he shall not see the good that I shall do to my people,

[1] 1(3) Kg 21:20–22, 29

[2] 2(4) Kg 9:7–9, 25–26 ; 10:1–11

[3] Num 16 ; 1–33

[4] Jos 7:1–26. Jos 22:20 mentions others as perishing besides Achan on account of the divine anger brought on Israel by reason of the transgression. This clearly refers to those slain by the men of Ai in a defeat attributed to Achan's sin, Jos 7:11f. Among those who consider that Achan's family perished with him, may be mentioned G. A. Barton, ERE II 479*a*, A. Fernandez, S.J., *Comm. in Libr. Josue* (Parisiis 1938 ; Cursus Scripturae Sacrae) 105, H. Wheeler Robinson in *The People and the Book* ed. A. S. Peake (Oxford 1925) 377, J. Ruwet, S.J., in VD 25 (1947) 91, A. Gelin, *Idées*, 50. E. Power, S.J., however, thinks that Achan alone was put to death. He points out rightly that the Hebrew text of Jos 7:25 has suffered in transmission and that the LXX mentions only the stoning of Achan. He also considers the mention of sons and daughters in 24 to be an early interpolation, CC, §231*b*.

[5] 2 Sam 21:1–14

saith Yahweh, because he has spoken treason against Yahweh'.[1] Jeremias is sometimes spoken of as the prophet of individual responsibility, but, as is plain from this passage, the solidarity of the family was still strong in his time, and indeeed, as will appear below, much later in Jewish history.

Besides the solidarity proper to the natural unit of the family there was also recognised that of the city. This is well illustrated by the men of a city speaking of its inhabitants in the first person singular. Thus when the Ark of God was brought to the city of Ekron, they cried out 'They have brought the Ark of the God of Israel to me to slay me and my people'. Then having sent for the lords of the Philistines they said: 'Send away the Ark of the God of Israel, and let it return to its own place, and let it not kill me and my people'.[2] Similarly the wise woman of Abel used the first person singular when speaking to Joab in the name of her city, which had a great reputation for the wisdom of its inhabitants. She reproaches Joab with seeking to destroy 'a mother in Israel'.[3] The city is the mother of its inhabitants and they are the children of the city. Thus the citizens of Sion are spoken of as 'the daughter of Sion',[4] the citizens of Jerusalem as 'the daughter of Jerusalem',[5] the use of the singular stressing the bond of union uniting the inhabitants and their consequent collective rights and responsibilities. It is enacted in Deuteronomy that if it should be reported that the dwellers in an Israelite city had fallen away and adopted idolatrous cults and diligent inquiry should establish the truth of the report, then all the inhabitants of that city were to be slain at the edge of the sword and everything in the city was to be destroyed, even to the cattle.[6] The knowledge that no

[1] Jer 29:32

[2] 1 Sam 5:10f. This indication of the sense of unity and solidarity is eliminated in both the Douay Version and the Revised Version, which both substitute the first person plural for the first person singular. The Septuagint translators also accommodated the text to their way of thinking by substituting the plural for the singular of the Hebrew.

[3] 2 Sam 20:19

[4] Is 1:8, Mic 1:13, etc.

[5] 2(4) Kg 19:21, Lam 2:13

[6] Dt 13:12-17 (HT 13-18)

property of any kind could be acquired for personal enrichment from the doomed city would remove the temptation to form a hasty judgment for the benefit of those who carried the law into effect. Although he had no such motive of self-aggrandisement, Saul seems to have acted with excessive severity and little sense of justice when he carried out a similar sentence on the priestly city of Nobe (Nob), as according to the record he had only the very slenderest evidence of any collective conspiracy of the priests against himself.[1] A more pleasant effect of civic solidarity is provided by the intercessory dialogue of Abraham with God Almighty. He started by asking whether God would not spare Sodom if there were fifty just men in the city. And receiving a favourable answer to that petition, he proceeded to make the same intercession in favour of gradually decreasing numbers till finally he was assured that the presence of ten just men would suffice to ensure the safety of the whole population.[2] There are limits, however, to the beneficent protection of just men. Iniquity may reach such a pitch that the decree of punishment is inevitable. So Ezechiel received a divine message that a land against which God's hand had been stretched out, could not be spared though three men most famous for their virtue were among the inhabitants. They would save their own lives but would not avail for the protection of the wicked.[3]

Comprising in itself all the lesser unities of family and city is the wider unit of the nation. In so far as its members

[1] 1 Sam 22:19 [2] Gen 18:23-32

[3] Ez 14:12-20. Two of the three are Noe and Job. The name of the third given in our texts as Daniel is not written in the consonantal Hebrew in the same way as that of the prophet but in a form which suggests the reading Danel. The prophet Daniel was a contemporary of Ezechiel's, and it has long been recognised as strange that he should be named together with the other two. Hence the old suggestion that an unknown person was here referred to. This suggestion has now been strikingly confirmed by the discovery of a personage named Danel and famed for justice in the Phoenician literature of Ugarit (Ras Shamra). As E. Power, S.J., writes in CC §484*j*: 'Most moderns accept the association of the Phoenician Danel with the Edomite Job. It may be assumed that Danel was an ancient historical figure, introduced into Phoenician mythology as Job was introduced into Hebrew Wisdom literature'.

are of the same race, it forms like the family a natural unit and its solidarity follows inevitably therefrom. In the case of Israel to this natural bond was added that of religion. And this religious bond sprang not merely from the fact that all Israelites worshipped the same one true God, but further from the consciousness that their race and theirs alone had been chosen out by God to be His own people in a quite peculiar way. This sense of national solidarity shows itself in the use by representatives of the nation of the first person singular and of words speaking of all as one. Thus when Moses sent messengers from Qadesh to the king of Edom requesting permission to pass through his territory, their message began 'Thus saith thy brother Israel'. Then after various sentences in which the first person plural is used, whereby the multiplicity of the members of the nation is recognised, follows the refusal of the Edomite king: 'Thou shalt not pass through me! If thou dost, I will march out with the sword to meet thee'. Israel insisted with a further message: 'We will go by the high way, and if we drink of thy waters, I and my cattle, I will give the price thereof. It is no great matter; only let me pass through'.[1]

The same unity is manifested in addresses of God to the nation by the use of the second person singular. Thus the Decalogue is introduced by the words 'I am Yahweh thy God who brought thee forth out of the land of Egypt, out of the house of bondage'. This shows that 'the first commandment with a promise', as St Paul calls it, though couched in the singular, is addressed to all: 'Honour thy father and thy mother that thy days may be long upon the land which Yahweh thy God will give thee'.[2] And the meaning is not that individual Israelites should be long-lived but that the nation might long enjoy the possession of the promised land. In the same way the long list of blessings and curses in Deuteronomy chap. 28 is addressed to the nation in the second person singular. For instance it is foretold that if the people will not listen to the voice of God and will not obey His

[1] Num 20:14–19. So also Num 21:2
[2] Ex 20:1, 12, Eph 6:2. See also Dt 5:6, 16

commandments, 'the heaven that is above thy head shall be of brass and the earth under thy feet of iron', Dt 28:23. Under such conditions, with no rain and the earth dry and hard, there would be no crops and famine would be the inevitable result. Now this penalty would fall upon the nation as a whole, and all its members would suffer. But, though the nation as a whole became godless, it would not be the case that each and every Israelite would have abandoned God. There would always be some faithful souls, as in the days of Elias, when the Northern Kingdom had given itself to idolatry, God said to the prophet 'I will leave seven thousand men in Israel whose knees have not been bowed before Baal'.[1] Such a situation clearly means that the innocent would suffer with the guilty; but whereas the suffering would be a punishment in the case of the guilty, it would not be a punishment in the case of the innocent. They would be involved in the common lot, not for any fault of their own, but by reason of the solidarity of the nation. This is an inevitable result of the constitution of the human family. What the wicked have called down upon themselves as retribution is for the just an occasion of the practice of virtue, of patience, of resignation, of trust in God, of charity to others overtaken by the calamity.

The king, as representative of the nation and embodying its corporate personality in himself, has the closest ties of solidarity with it. The result of this is that the acts of the king are in a measure the acts of the nation, and the whole nation may be involved in the evil consequences of the actions of their rulers. Thus there was a three-year famine in the days of David 'on account of Saul and his blood-stained house'.[2] So also the people suffered by reason of the sin of King David in numbering the nation.[3] In the religious sphere the representative of the nation was the high-priest and his wrong-doing could 'bring guilt upon the people', that is, could involve the people in the guilt of his own act.[4] So too if any of the tribes sinned, their transgression could cause the

[1] 1(3) Kg 19:18
[2] 2 Sam 21:1
[3] 2 Sam 24:1–17
[4] Lev 4:3

wrath of God to 'rage against all Israel'.[1] Even the grave misdemeanour of one Israelite could implicate all, as is shown in the story of Achan.[2]

In the light of this principle of solidarity we must now consider a passage which occurs in the context of the Decalogue. After the prohibition of idolatry the text continues: 'I am Yahweh thy God, a jealous God, visiting the iniquities of the fathers upon the children unto the third and fourth generation of them that hate me, and showing mercy to the thousandth (generation) of them that love me and keep my commandments'.[3] With this must be taken the following text, also from Exodus—the words are those of Moses addressing God: 'O Yahweh, O God merciful and gracious, patient and of much compassion and faithful, who keepest mercy unto the thousandth (generation), who takest away iniquity and wickedness and sin, but wilt not declare (the guilty) innocent, visiting the iniquity of the fathers upon the children and upon the children's children unto the third and fourth generation'.[4] First a word of explanation concerning the translation offered. Where this has 'showing mercy to the thousandth generation' both the Douay Version and the Revised Version have 'showing mercy unto thousands', a translation which the words considered apart from the context will certainly bear. But in the context the words come as an antithesis to 'the third and fourth generation', and whereas the Hebrew language has special words to denote the third and fourth generations, it has no special form to signify the thousandth and is obliged to use the cardinal number with resulting ambiguity. But here the antithesis clearly postulates a reference to the thousandth generation.[5] And this is borne out by the text of Deuteronomy which speaks explicitly of God as 'keeping his covenant and mercy to them that love him and to them that observe his commandments unto a thousand generations'.[6] These words give an authentic interpretation of the previous

[1] Jos 22:18 [2] Jos 7:1, 11, 18; 22:20 [3] Ex 20:5f.
[4] Ex 34:6f. See also Num 14:18, Dt 5:9f.
[5] This is noted in a work attributed to St Athanasius, *De communi essentia Patris et Filii et Spiritus Sancti*, Migne, PG 28:72
[6] Dt 7:9

passage. Hence the contrast is between the third and fourth generations, a period which as noted by Cornelius a Lapide,[1] practically corresponds to the possible length of the fathers' lives and the persistence of the memory of their iniquities, and a thousand generations. The passage, therefore, while alluding to God's retributive justice, puts great emphasis on His mercy and forgiveness. Secondly, the passage speaks of the nation as a whole, and not of individual families. The context is that of the Decalogue, which is addressed, as we have seen, p. 65, in the second person singular, not to individuals, but to the whole nation. And the evil deeds of one generation can bring disastrous results for its posterity, as in the case of an unjust war. These disastrous results are not a punishment of the posterity but a consequence of the solidarity of the nation. But,[2] thirdly, the passage speaks rather of a guilty posterity and of an innocent posterity respectively, ' of them that hate me ' and ' of them that love me '. Thus the question arises in what sense a guilty posterity is visited with the guilt of its fathers ? No generation receives more severe punishment than it deserves. That is an elementary rule of justice. On the contrary, God, who is ' patient and of much compassion ', often does not inflict such punishment as is deserved. But if in spite of God's long-suffering a nation persists in its evil ways, the patience of God, to speak in human terms, becomes exhausted. He no longer extends His mercy to that nation ; the cup of their iniquity is full [3] and He allows to fall on them the full measure of the penalty they deserve. This again is an effect of the solidarity of the nation which exists not only between men living together at the same time but also between successive generations of the same nation. Thus no generation is punished more severely than its own wickedness deserves, but its punishment may be more severe than it would have been, had not the persistent wickedness of

[1] Comment on Dt 5:9

[2] Peake, *Problem*, 21 : ' The old saying is true that the sins of the fathers are visited on the children. We are members one of another, no man lives to himself, our character and conduct alike are largely determined, for good or ill, by forces in whose release we had no share '.

[3] Gen 15:16

previous generations shown that the nation is no longer worthy or rather is no longer even a fit recipient of God's mercy and compassion. In this sense our Lord said that there would come upon the Jews of His time 'all the just blood that hath been shed upon the earth, from the blood of Abel the just even unto the blood of Zacharias . . . whom you killed between the temple and the altar. Amen I say to you, all these things shall come upon this generation'.[1] When Moses foretold the punishment that would overtake infidelity to God and His law, he said: 'They shall pine away in their iniquity in the land of their enemies and they shall pine away for the iniquities of their fathers and their own, until they confess their iniquity and the iniquity of their fathers, whereby they have transgressed against me and walked contrary to me'.[2] Here again the sorrows of exile are the cumulative effect of long-protracted iniquity and illustrate the truth that God is 'patient and of much compassion'.[3]

Finally, as an instance of the children bearing the iniquities of the fathers and in a national, not individual, sense, may be mentioned the penalty inflicted on the generation of adults who escaped out of Egypt. Because of their murmuring and distrust of God those of them who had attained the age of twenty years and upward were not allowed to share the privilege of entering into possession of the promised land. 'But your children, of whom you said that they would become a prey, will I bring in that they may see the land which you have despised, but your carcasses shall lie in this wilderness. Your children shall wander in the desert forty years and shall bear your fornications until your carcasses be consumed in the desert'.[4]

These considerations on the solidarity subsisting between the members of various groups, whether natural or purely social, between the members of family, city, and nation, help to an understanding of the fact that suffering, which for some is a punishment, may for others be nothing but the natural consequence of membership of such a group. The distinction is admittedly subtle, and it may be objected that the sufferings

[1] Mt 23:35f.
[2] Lev 26:39f.
[3] Ex 34:6
[4] Num 14:28–33

endured may be exactly the same for the innocent as for the guilty. This may well be true as it may be in the case of a criminal taken to execution for his heinous misdeeds and a martyr enduring the death-sentence for his adherence to the true Faith and refusal to offer incense to idols. And this consideration is a help to a clearer understanding of the validity of the distinction. Our feelings for the one and for the other are entirely different. Our commiseration for the criminal is tempered by the knowledge that he is suffering a penalty justly inflicted by law and that he has brought his lot upon himself by acts fully deserving of it. For the martyr, on the other hand, our feelings are of admiration rather than of commiseration. We know that many a holy soul has prayed for the grace of martyrdom and that the martyr has the glory of giving his life for God and for his Faith. The mind of the Hebrews, however, was practical and not speculative. It was religious but neither theological nor philosophical. And hence distinctions which seem obvious to us after centuries of developed theology, were not so to them, and they do not seem to have explicitly grasped this difference between suffering as a penalty and suffering as an unavoidable concomitant of the conditions of human existence. These considerations also help us to understand how the human race could be involved in the consequences of the rejection of God's service by their first parent. His act, as that of the head and representative of the race, had its repercussion on all.

E. Ehrhardt has written on 'Solidarity' from a general point of view in ERE XI 677f., where he gives references to further literature. Of writers treating of the subject from the biblical side may be mentioned: H. Wheeler Robinson, 'Human Psychology' in *The People and the Book*, ed. A. S. Peake (Oxford 1925), 375–80; also 'The Hebrew Conception of Corporate Personality' in *Werden und Wesen des Alten Testaments*, herausgegeben von J. Hempel (Berlin 1936; BZAW 66), 49–62; O. Eissfeldt, ET 44 (1932/3), 264–8; A. R. Johnson, *The One and the Many in the Israelite Conception of God* (Cardiff 1942); R. Gordis, 'Corporate Personality in

Job : a Note on 22:29–30 ', JNES 4 (1945), 54f. ; J. Ruwet, S.J., 'Misericordia et Iustitia Dei in Vetere Testamento ', VD 25 (1947), 89–98 ; A. Gelin, *Idées*, 49–53 ; C. Lattey, S.J., 'Vicarious Solidarity in the Old Testament ', VT 1 (1951), 267–74 ; J. de Fraine, *Biblica* 33 (1952), 339f.

Chapter V

THE DOCTRINE OF THE PSALMS

In the psalms we have the outpouring of the devotion and the expression of the beliefs of the Israelites, and their sanction is that of inspiration and authoritative admission to the canon of sacred writings. Now the Israelites knew that God is both omnipotent and just. Because He is omnipotent, He can do what He will: 'Is anything too hard for Yahweh?'[1] And because He is just, He cannot will except what is in accord with the norm of right: 'God is a just judge'.[2] Moreover, He is not a Creator who disinterests Himself in the world He created. The whole course of sacred history cries out against such a thought. From the Garden of Eden onwards every page of the Bible represents God as the diligent guardian of the moral order. Therefore the Hebrews knew that God rewards the virtuous and punishes the wicked. But for the greater part of their history they had no knowledge of retribution beyond the grave by which the inequalities of this world can be rectified.[3] Consequently their thoughts were confined to God's government of this world and they looked for the rewards and punishments of the good and the wicked during men's lifetime. The conception is radically sound as formulating the important truths just indicated that God is omnipotent, just, and the faithful guardian of right. It is at the same time incomplete. It is voiced with earnest faith in several of the Psalms, for instance in Ps 111(112):

Happy the man with reverence for Yahweh,
  Whose great delight is in his commands.
Mighty in the land shall be his seed;
  A blessing shall rest on a righteous generation.[4]

[1] Gen 18:14 [2] Ps 7:12 [3] Sutcliffe, *Future Life*
[4] As indicated by the parallelism the righteous generation are those called the seed of the virtuous man in the first half of this verse.

Wealth and riches shall be in his house,
And his prosperity abideth for ever.[1]

A light ariseth for the upright in times of darkness[2];
The just man is merciful and compassionate.
Good is the compassionate man who lendeth,
Who disposeth his affairs with justice
Never indeed shall the just be overthrown;
In perpetual remembrance shall he be.
No evil report shall cause him fear;
His heart is established trusting in Yahweh.
His heart sustained shall not need to fear,
Until he seeth his joy upon his enemies.

He giveth largess to the poor[3];
His prosperity abideth for ever.[1]
His horn is exalted in glory[4];
The wicked man shall be vexed at the sight.
He shall gnash his teeth and pine;
The desire of the wicked shall come to nought.

Similar is the theme of Ps 127(128):

Happy are all who reverence Yahweh,
Who walk in his ways.
Of the toil of thy hands thou shalt eat.[5]
Happy art thou and it shall be well with thee.

[1] The word translated 'prosperity' means literally 'justice', and is here used in its secondary sense of the effect or reward of justice.

[2] Darkness or dark times is an expression symbolical of trial and distress, and light of the opposite.

[3] The underlying idea is that the virtuous man has the wherewithal to be generous.

[4] The horn is the symbol of power and success.

[5] Here is another instance of a word used to signify the effect of that signified by the word itself, 'toil' standing for the produce of toil in field or garden. The implication of the line is double, firstly, that the toil would be blessed and productive, and, secondly, that the produce of the toil would not be consumed by enemies or invading armies. The same thought occurs in Is 65:21–22: 'they shall plant vineyards and shall eat the fruit thereof . . . they shall not plant and another eat'.

Thy wife is like a fruitful vine
  In the inner parts of thy house.[1]
Thy children are like olive saplings
  Round about thy table.
Lo ! Such are the blessings of the man
  With reverence for Yahweh.
Yahweh shall bless thee from Sion
  And thou shalt enjoy the good things of Jerusalem
  All the days of thy life.
And thou shalt see thy children's children.
  Peace be upon Israel !

The same theme of the contrasted lot of the just and the wicked is treated in Ps 90(91). Of the latter it is said, 8 :

Thou shalt behold with thine eyes
  And shalt see the retribution of the wicked.

And of the former, 10–12 :

There shall no evil befall thee,
  Nor shall the scourge come nigh thy tent.
For he has given his angels charge over thee
  To keep thee in all thy ways.
In their hands shall they bear thee up,
  Lest thou dash thy foot against a stone.

Now it would be a mistake to suppose that these psalms are laying down absolute and immutable laws of divine providence. It is true that the statements are expressed without qualification as if they were of universal application admitting of no exception. But the character of the biblical writings must be borne in mind. They are not theological treatises in which the terms of every assertion are carefully selected in

[1] His wife will be a mother blessed with numerous children, and, moreover, she will be a faithful wife, attentive to her duties in the house and avoiding the restless habit of unnecessarily 'going about from house to house', which St Paul condemns in young widows, 1 Tim 5:13.

order to take due account of all known aspects of the subject treated, and qualifying clauses are added to forestall improper extension of the truth enunciated. The psalms are popular religious compositions written in accordance with the genius of the Hebrew mentality. For the human characteristics of the sacred writers are not eliminated by inspiration. On the contrary, God, again to speak in human fashion, accommodated Himself to the modes of thought and speech of the writers He inspired. Now, it is a characteristic of Hebrew writers to stress the thought and lesson in hand as if it comprised the whole truth and as if it were of universal validity. This may be illustrated from the sayings of our Blessed Lord Himself. On one occasion when He was warning the disciples of the sufferings and persecutions which awaited them, He said: 'Do not think that I came to send peace upon earth; I came not to send peace but the sword'.[1] How far from understanding the character of Christ and the purpose of His mission would he be who imagined this to express the whole truth about His intentions. No, these words must be understood in the light of what He said elsewhere: 'Peace I leave with you; my peace I give unto you; not as the world giveth do I give unto you. Let not your heart be troubled nor let it be afraid'.[2] This habit of the biblical writers was noticed long ago by St Augustine and he expressed it in the words: 'It is the wont of Holy Scripture to treat of the part as if it were the whole'.[3] He was not thinking of measurable quantities but of themes such as that here under discussion. Here too one aspect of the matter is stressed, namely, that God protects and rewards the just; but for a fuller understanding of this biblical teaching we must consider other passages as well.

Ps 36(37) stresses the same teaching as the two psalms just considered, but its opening verse shows the supposition to be quite false that those two psalms imply perpetual misfortune for the wicked. Here the psalmist starts from the experience that often the unjust do prosper and he warns his hearers or

[1] Mt 10:34 [2] Jn 14:27
[3] *Epistola ad Paulinum* 149 (*al.* 59), CSEL, *Aug. Epist.* III 366; Migne, PL 33:638

readers not to be disturbed by the fact, for this prosperity cannot be permanent.

> Be not moved to anger against the wicked ;
>   Do not be zealous against the workers of iniquity ;
> For like the grass they shall quickly wither
>   And like the green herbage shall wilt away.

In Palestine when the rains of spring are succeeded by the hot sun of summer, the vegetation quickly withers. In the psalm it is several times said that those faithful to God shall inherit the land. The meaning is that they will share in the blessing by which God promised His chosen people possession of the land of Canaan. In verse 25 the psalmist says :

> I have been young and now am old ;
>   Yet have I not seen the just man forsaken
>   Nor his seed seeking bread.

This may represent the actual experience of his life, but the use of hyperbole cannot be excluded. An example of this figure of speech is found in the prophet Micheas, 7:2 : 'The pious man is perished out of the land and there is none upright among men'. Certainly the prophet himself must be excluded and Isaias, his contemporary ; and no doubt there were not wanting other God-fearing Israelites at the time.[1]

Ps 37(38) comes from the pen of a man enduring great pains of body and troubled in mind. He is abandoned by friends and relatives and is exposed to the attacks of bitter enemies. In face of their malicious talk against him he shows remarkable patience and resignation :

> But I am like a deaf man that heareth not
>   And like a dumb man that openeth not his mouth ;
> And I have been as a man that heareth not,
>   In whose mouth are no reproaches.

[1] A translation of this psalm with comments may be found in Sutcliffe, *Future Life*, 95ff.

He humbly acknowledges that his tribulations are 'on account of my sins'.

> I will declare my iniquity ;
> I will repent of my sin.

He ends by begging God not to forsake him but to hasten to his aid.

Ps 38(39) is in many ways similar to the preceding. Here again the psalmist is suffering severely and feels himself close to death. He acknowledges his wrong-doing : 'Deliver me from all my transgressions'. And he is resigned because he recognises in his afflictions the hand of God :

> I was dumb, not opening my mouth,
> Because thou hast done it.

And again, 'By reproaches for iniquity thou dost correct a man'. Here by reproaches can hardly be meant anything other than the sufferings he is enduring. These afflictions are God's reproaches in act. This is a new thought regarding the function of misfortune and suffering. They are not merely penalties inflicted in retribution for wrong done ; they are also medicinal, giving a man occasion to enter into himself, to reflect on his conduct, and to see the values of life from the standpoint of religion. The opening of the psalm contains another reflection which is not present in the preceding one. The sufferer finds himself in the presence of a wicked man, and he cannot help contrasting his lot with that of this man who is openly contemptuous of God's law. He feels his indignation hot within him, but determines to keep a guard on his mouth lest he give utterance to a thought unworthy of one conscious of God's claims upon him. In prayer he grows calm and confesses that God alone is his true helper :

> And now for what do I wait, O Lord ?
> My hope is in thee.

And he means that it is in God alone and nowhere else.

Riches form the theme also of Ps 48(49) and its importance

is indicated by the preliminary appeal to all persons whatsoever to give ear and attend, as the matter is of consequence to high and low, to ' rich and poor '.

> Why should I fear in times of evil,
> When encompassed by the iniquity of insidious men,
> Who trust in their wealth
> And glory in the abundance of their riches ?

It is to be noted that as in Ps 38(39) it is tacitly assumed that the wicked man is also wealthy, so here the rich are assumed to be wicked. Indeed, the two terms ' rich ' and ' wicked ' are almost synonymous.[1] The words of our Lord come to mind, ' A rich man shall enter with difficulty into the kingdom of heaven '.[2] The feebleness of riches is demonstrated in the psalm by their inability to save their possessor from the common law of death. No matter how great a man's wealth may be, it cannot provide a price at which he can buy a right to continued life. No, the rich die and must ' leave their wealth to others '.

> Their tomb is their home for ever,
> Their dwelling-place to generation and generation.

Again the psalmist returns to the powerlessness of men in face of death :

> Like a flock of sheep Death controls them ;
> They go straight down to the grave.[3]

[1] See for instance Job 21:28, Wis 2:10. This fact, the realisation of which aids the understanding of various passages, has been pointed out by several writers. M. Buttenwieser, *The Book of Job* (London 1922) 256 writes : ' These critics miss the very essential point that for Job the rich who got their wealth through the exploitation of the poor were the wicked. . . . This viewpoint grew out of the preaching of the prophets, who in their denunciation of the social injustice of their times described the rich as the unrighteous oppressors and the poor as the innocent sufferers '. Cf. Gelin, *Idées*, 72, J. Lindblom, ZAW 63 (1951) 245, L. G. Rignell, VT 3 (1953) 91.

[2] Mt 19:23

[3] This seems to be the true meaning of verse 15. Two words at the beginning are displaced from the close and the mention of Sheol, the home of the dead, is accidentally repeated. The second part of the verse as vocalised

Now the psalmist makes his profession of faith and trust in God. Wealth is powerless to redeem from death, not so the hand of God :

> But God will redeem my life ;
> From the power of Sheol indeed he will take me.

God, that is, can save from imminent death, and prevent His suppliant from falling under the control of Sheol. There is no thought here of God's resurrecting a person who has died and so fallen already into the power of Sheol.[1] The psalmist then returns to his theme of the insecure hold the rich man has on his wealth.

> In his death he can take nothing ;
> His glory cannot descend after him.

And again :

> He shall go to the generation of his forebears ;
> Never again shall they see the light.

Thus the solution offered by the psalm is incomplete. The rich man with all his wealth cannot save or prolong his life ; the just man can be saved from the danger of death by his trustful petition to God. The rich man has no permanence in the possession of his fortune ; at death he is separated from it for ever.

The 36(37)th psalm was written by a man whose serene faith hardly allowed him to recognise that the prosperity of the wicked presented a problem at all. In contrast to this the author of Ps 72(73) confesses that his religious foundations were for a time seriously shaken.

---

by the Massoretes reads : 'The just rule over them in the morning'. The text of the psalm is notoriously corrupt in places ; this sentence gives no intelligible sense in the context of the Old Testament ; and the same consonants, with the inversion of two, when differently vocalised give the meaning printed in the text, a meaning which suits the context and gives good parallelism to the first line. cf. R. Tournay, O.P., *Les Psaumes* (Paris 1950 ; La Sainte Bible de Jérusalem).

[1] On this question see Sutcliffe, *Future Life*, 99ff. ; R. Tournay, O.P., 'L'Eschatologie individuelle dans les Psaumes', RB 56 (1949) 496ff.

How good to the upright is God !
  How good is he to the pure of heart !
Yet my own foothold was well-nigh lost ;
  My feet had almost gone astray.
For I was envious of the foolish,
  When I saw the prosperity of the wicked.

The psalmist then describes their prosperity and immunity from the hardships which beset the mass of men. Their privileged condition makes them proud and arrogant. They oppress their weaker brethren and their words show regard neither for God nor for man. Conscious of their successful combination of sinfulness and prosperity they infer that God cannot know what passes on earth :

And they say 'How does God know ?'
  And 'Is there knowledge in the most High ?'
Lo ! Such are the wicked,
  And in constant peace they multiply their substance.

Then comes the psalmist's temptation against the practice of religion :

Surely for nothing have I kept my heart pure
  And washed my hands in innocence.

For in spite of his moral life he had been constantly plagued and met new trials every day. But he stayed himself by the thought that to adopt the attitude of the impious would be to abandon the faith of Israel in God. So he determined to penetrate the mystery, painful though he found the effort. Then comprehension came to him in the thought of the end met by these men.

Verily in slippery places dost thou set them,
  And so thou dost cast them down to destruction.
How in a moment are they become a desolation !
  Terrors complete their destruction.

When my heart was embittered
  And my reins pierced,
I was brutish and without knowledge ;
  I was like a beast in thy presence.

The psalmist now gives expression to his sense of intimate friendship with God in a passage which has few parallels in the Old Testament for its sublimity.

I am always with thee ;
  Thou hast my right hand in thy grasp.
With thy counsel thou dost guide me,
  And with glory wilt thou take me.[1]
Whom have I in heaven (but thee) ?
  And besides thee have I no pleasure on earth.

This beautiful passage may be summed up in the words of the psalm : 'God is my portion for ever', and again 'For me it is good to be near to God'. Here the psalmist reaches a profound and deeply religious solution of the problem that troubled him though not one that touches on all its aspects. He is convinced that in the love of God and intimacy with God he has a treasure surpassing the possession of earthly

[1] So the Septuagint except that there the verb is in the past tense. The verb for 'take' is as common in Hebrew as in English. It occurs, for instance, in Ps 17(18):17 : 'He sends from on high to take me ; he draws me out of mighty waters', that is, out of grave affliction and danger. There is nothing in the psalm to suggest that the psalmist had in mind the rewards of the world to come. These were unknown in Israel till the closing centuries before Christ. Had the writer in fact intended to explain the inequalities of life by the rewards and punishments of the life beyond the grave, he would not have introduced this entirely new and epoch-making thought in a passing and obscurely-worded reference. The expression 'for ever' in the sentence 'God is my portion for ever' does not of itself point to a time after the cessation of earthly life. So, for instance, 'May my lord King David live for ever', 1(3) Kg 1:31. The psalmist's sense of intimacy with God and the desire never to be parted from Him, shared, as it no doubt was, by other pious Israelites, will have been one of the forces working to give birth in course of time to the belief in a happy immortality in the presence of God in heaven. For a fuller consideration and rejection of the view that our psalmist had such a thought in mind the reader may be referred to Sutcliffe, *Future Life*, 102–8 and R. Tournay, O.P., 'L'Eschatologie individuelle dans les Psaumes', RB 56 (1949) 496ff.

riches however great. Riches are insecure; the moth consumes, the robber robs. But intimacy with God is a treasure no man can take from His friends.

Not all, however, had the strong love and faith of this psalmist; and the immunity of the violators of God's law provided a temptation to which many succumbed. They drew the conclusion that God in His high heaven knew nothing of the actions of men and that therefore they were free to pursue their evil ways without fear of divine chastisement. These men were deists, both speculative and practical. They did not think of denying His existence, but they denied that His providence exercised any control over the course of events on this earth. Isaias is scornful of such opinions: 'Woe to you that are deep of heart, to hide your counsel from the Lord! And their works are in the dark, and they say: Who seeth us, and who knoweth us? This is your perversity! Is the potter to be reckoned as clay that the work should say of its maker, He has not made me, or the thing fashioned should say of him that fashioned it He hath no understanding.[1] So too we read in the Book of Ezechiel that the Lord said to him: 'The iniquity of the house of Israel and of Judah is exceeding great and excessive, and the land is filled with blood and the city is filled with justice perverted; for they say Yahweh hath forsaken the land and Yahweh seeth not.'[2] There are various echoes of this mentality in the psalms. The wicked man is said to spurn God and in his lofty anger to exclaim 'He will not requite' and 'There is no God'.[3] As the combination of the two statements shows, the second is not a denial of the existence of God, for this is supposed and admitted in the first. The word *Elohim*, that here used for 'God', has not infrequently the pregnant sense of 'God active with His protecting providence' whether with regard to the nation or individual persons. And this is the sense here. The meaning, therefore, is 'God is not concerned with the actions of men, whether good or bad'; and the conclusion from this is that men are under no restraint and

[1] Is 29:15f. [2] Ez 9:9; cp. 8:12
[3] Ps 10:4 (Hebrew numeration)

can do with impunity whatever they please. That this is the correct meaning of the statement is shown further by verse 11:

> He saith in his heart 'God has forgotten;
> He has hidden his face and seeth nothing'.

This is the meaning also in Ps 13(14):1:

> The fool has said in his heart:
> 'There is no God.'

And the result of this attitude is what might be expected: 'Their ways are corrupt and abominable; there is not one that doth good'. Again the men who spoke lies to each other 'with flattering lips and duplicity at heart' claimed complete moral independence: 'Our tongues are our own; who is Lord over us?'[1] The quotation of one or two more passages will bring into relief the number of those whose wickedness was fostered by this false conception of God. Another psalm speaks of 'workers of iniquity, blood-stained men', who adopted a similar refrain: 'Who doth hear?' And the psalmist prays to God:

> Consume them in wrath, consume them, that they be no more;
> And let them know that God doth rule
> In Jacob and to the ends of the earth.[2]

Similarly of evildoers who planned to lay snares to catch the unwary, a psalmist says 'they encourage themselves with evil talk . . . Who shall see us?' But God, he says, will take action against them. And, when God's action is manifest—

> All men shall fear
> And shall tell of God's action
> And shall comprehend his act.[3]

[1] Ps 11(12):3, 5 [2] Ps 58(59):3, 8, 14
[3] Ps 63(64):6, 10. The Hebrew text has 'Who shall see them?', but the version of St Jerome (from the Hebrew) and the Syriac translation are doubtless right in using the first person plural as in the translation above.

When God thus intervenes, men will see the folly of the position adopted by the deists and will be filled with a holy fear of His justice.

Finally in this connection may be quoted the opening verses of Psalm 93 (94) :

O thou avenging God, Yahweh,
  O thou avenging God, manifest thyself !
Be thou exalted, O thou ruler of the earth !
  Requite their recompense unto the proud !
How long shall the wicked, O Yahweh,
  How long shall the wicked exult ?
How long shall they give vent to arrogant talk
  And flout themselves, all workers of iniquity ?
It is thy people, Yahweh, whom they crush
  And thine inheritance that they oppress.
The widow and the stranger they murder
  And orphans they slay.
Yet they say ' Yahweh doth not see
  And the God of Jacob payeth no regard '.
Have understanding, ye most senseless men,
  And ye foolish, when will ye be wise ?
He who implanted the ear, cannot he hear ?
  Can he who fashioned the eye, not perceive,
Can he who chastens the nations, not rebuke,
  He who instructs man, has he no knowledge ? [1]
Yahweh knows the thoughts of man,
  That they are vanity.[1]

Rather strangely Eliphaz the Temanite accuses Job of holding this same opinion :

Is not God on high in heaven
  And doth he not look upon the stars aloft ?
And so thou thinkest ' What doth God know ?
  Can he judge behind a dark cloud ?

[1] Ps 93 (94):1–11. The words ' has he no knowledge ' represent a small correction of the Hebrew text demanded by the sense.

Clouds are his covert, and he cannot see ;
He walketh on the vault of heaven '.[1]

God's dwelling is so far elevated above this earth of ours where men live as to suggest that what happens here is beyond the range of his knowledge. The reference to the dark cloud is based on earlier passages of the Old Testament. In the theophany of Sinai, God spoke to Moses from a dark cloud.[2] So too at Solomon's dedication of the temple God manifested His presence in the same way.[3] And a psalmist writes : ' Clouds and darkness are round about him ', which in poetic language describes God's invisiblity and His physical inaccessibility to men.[4] In the speech of Eliphaz the image is understood in the opposite sense that this dark cloud obscures God's vision and hides from Him the doings of men. Actually Job had not uttered any such thought. He had said the contrary :

If I sinned, thou wouldst set a watch upon me
And wouldst not acquit me of my iniquity.[5]

And again, on the impossible supposition that Job could take refuge in Sheol until God's anger had passed and then return to earth, he says :

For then thou wouldst count my steps
And wouldst not keep watch for my sin.[6]

Yet Eliphaz had this justification that in his immediately preceding speech Job did speak of the lot of men in this world in a way which at least gave ground for supposing that he had in mind the thought attributed to him. He depicts at length the happy lot of the wicked.

Why do the wicked live ?
Why do they prosper, even wax mighty in wealth ? [7]

[1] Job 22:12–14
[2] Ex 20:21
[3] 1(3) Kg 8:11f.
[4] Ps 96(97):2
[5] Job 10:14
[6] Job 14:16
[7] Job 21:7

How often is the lamp of the wicked extinguished ?
And how often does the calamity they merit come upon them ?[1]

And he goes on to say that without apparent reason the life of one knows nothing but success and happiness, whereas another meets with nothing but want and misery. However, whatever justification there may be for the accusation against Job, the passage further illustrates how readily the thought could occur to the mind of reflective Israelites.

This brings to an end our survey of the problem of suffering as seen in the psalms. The prevalent view was that God, as the just and omnipotent guardian of the moral order, visits the sinner with punishment and protects and rewards the good. But the doctrine, true as it is, remained incomplete for the reason that God's providence had not revealed the further truth that divine retribution is largely reserved for the life after death. Hence the apparent inequalities of life presented a problem capable of disturbing the faith even of God-fearing men. A partial solution was found in the medicinal value of suffering, which gives opportunity for reflection, repentance, and amendment of life. And religious souls were content to abide in the intimacy of God, to put their trust in Him, confident that His ways are just even though their own minds were incapable of full comprehension. On the other hand, many men who had given themselves over to the delights of power and wealth regardless of the rights of their fellow-men, found in these same inequalities of life an argument to lull themselves into a false sense of security as if God, the Creator of the world, had no concern for the behaviour of His creatures.

[1] Job 21:17

Chapter VI

INDIVIDUAL RETRIBUTION

The consideration of corporate personality and corporate retribution which formed the subject of a previous chapter, remains to be amplified in the light of certain other texts. This further consideration will, however, be more conveniently deferred till after a review of passages dealing with individual rewards and punishments. The blessings promised in the Pentateuch for the faithful observance of God's law and the curses there pronounced against its transgressors are in large measure addressed to the nation as a whole. Even the Decalogue, the observance of which is the duty of each individual member of the community, is nevertheless, as we have seen, p. 65, imposed as an obligation, not directly on these separate members, but on the community as a whole, and only through the community on its members. And this is true also of the one promise which it contains. And the reason for this direct address to the community is that the Covenant into which God was entering and which we designate by the name of the Old Testament, was a Covenant not with individual Israelites but with the nation of Israel. It was the nation which God chose to be His own in a very special way and it was only through the nation and as members of the nation that individual Israelites shared in the privileges of the Covenant.

Still even in the Pentateuch individual responsibility and individual retribution are by no means lost sight of. In the original Sinaitic legislation various crimes are punished by the death sentence. To give a few examples : the homicide who strikes another and thereby causes his death, anyone who strikes his father or mother, anyone who steals a man and sells him (into slavery), anyone who curses his father or mother—all these are to be put to death.[1] By the execution of the

[1] Ex 21:12, 15, 16, 17

death sentence the guilty member of the community is punished personally, the moral rectitude of the community itself is safeguarded by the exclusion of an offending and sinful member and by the salutary warning it conveyed to the survivors. In this way these laws subserved the divine purpose that Israel should be 'a holy nation'.[1] In the Book of Numbers it is laid down in general that all offences committed intentionally and with deliberate contempt of the law are deserving of excommunication from the community: 'The person who committeth anything with a high hand, whether born in the land or a stranger, acts contumeliously against Yahweh and shall be cut off from among his people'.[2]

In addition to these legislative pronouncements the Pentateuch contains examples of individual retribution and some of these are related from the earliest times. It is thus clear that side by side with the prominence national retribution receives in the records of Israel the thought of individual retribution can never have been unknown or forgotten. Noe was saved out of the midst of the corruption universally reigning in his day.[3] Lot and his family were rescued from the destruction of the cities of the plain, and, if his wife was overtaken by the calamity while on the way to safety, it was because of her own disobedience to orders received.[4] Miriam, Moses' sister, was severely punished for her rebellious and proud speech against Moses, the leader chosen and appointed by God.[5] The man found violating the sanctity of the Sabbath in the wilderness was stoned to death by divine instruction.[6] Josue and Caleb were exempted from the sentence by which the generation which came out of Egypt aged twenty and upwards, lost the privilege of ever seeing and entering the promised land.[7] Phineas received a special blessing for the zeal he

[1] Ex 19:6

[2] Num 15:30. The Douay Version translates according to the sense and substitutes 'through pride' for the Hebrew expression 'with a high hand'. For such sins no sacrificial expiation is allowed. The Revised Version uses the phrase 'blasphemeth the Lord', but there is no mention of spoken words, and the context demands rather 'acts contumeliously against'.

[3] Gen chapters 6–7

[4] Gen 19:15–26

[5] Num 12:1–15

[6] Num 15:32–36

[7] Num 14:6–10, 26–30

manifested for the honour of God.[1] Jeroboam, the first monarch of the Northern Kingdom, when he was offering incense upon his new altar at Bethel and refused to listen to the word of the Lord sent by a man of God, was at once punished by the withering of his hand.[2] And when Ozias had the temerity to usurp the sacerdotal function of offering incense upon the altar of incense in the temple, he was at once struck with leprosy in the sight of all and remained a leper until his death.[3] Thus both the law and various incidents provide abundant evidence that side by side with the concept of solidarity there was always present the knowledge of individual responsibility and retribution.

For the administration of human justice it was explicitly laid down in the law that 'Fathers shall not be put to death for their children nor children for their fathers, but each one shall die for his own sin'.[4] And when Amasias, the son of Joas, put to death the murderers who had conspired together and slain his father, it was out of deference to this law that he abstained from including their children in the sentence.[5] The existence of such a law is obviously itself an indication of the manner in which the Israelites were prone to execute justice. And the law was not always observed; but the non-observance of a law does not demonstrate its non-existence. And in general, it may be said, that the pages of Hebrew history show that the prescriptions of the Mosaic law were widely disregarded.

The examples already quoted from the earlier books of the Bible show that there is nothing new in the instances of individual responsibility recorded in the Book of Ezechiel. This prophet laboured in Babylonia during the first half of the sixth century B.C. He was warned by God of his own personal responsibility for the safety of those committed to his care as a prophet set to watch over the welfare of Israel. 'Son of man, I have made thee a watchman for the house of Israel; thou shalt hear the word out of my mouth and shalt tell it them

[1] Num 25:7–13
[2] 1(3) Kg 13:1–4
[3] 2 Par 26:16–21
[4] Dt 24:16
[5] 2(4) Kg 12:20; 14:5–6; 2 Par 24:25; 25:3f.

from me. If, when I say to the wicked "Thou shalt surely die", thou declare it not to him nor speak to him that he may be converted from his wicked way and live, the same wicked man shall die in his iniquity but I will require his blood at thy hand. But if thou give warning to the wicked and he be not converted from his wickedness and from his evil way, he indeed shall die in his iniquity but thou wilt have delivered thy soul'.[1] There follows the same warning in the case of the just man who should turn from his righteousness and begin to practise iniquity. In the vision of the destruction of Jerusalem vouchsafed to the prophet he saw a man 'clothed with linen and with a writer's inkhorn at his reins'. This man received orders from God : 'Go through the midst of the city, through the midst of Jerusalem, and mark a Tau upon the foreheads of the men that sigh and mourn for all the abominations that are committed in the midst thereof'.[2] All others were to be destroyed. Only those thus marked with the last letter of the Hebrew alphabet, which in the ancient script had the form of a cross, were to be spared.

What is new in the Book of Ezechiel is, therefore, not the application of the idea of individual responsibility but its theoretical elaboration. To this subject is devoted the whole of chapter 18. 'Behold, all souls are mine : as the soul of the father, so also the soul of the son is mine ; the soul that sinneth, the same shall die'. The man that 'hath walked in my commandments and kept my ordinances, to deal faithfully : he is just, he shall surely live, saith the Lord Yahweh. But if he beget a son that is a robber, a shedder of blood, and that hath done some one of these things, . . . he shall not live. Seeing he has done all these detestable things, he shall surely die ; his blood shall be upon him. But if he beget a son, who, seeing all his father's sins, which he hath committed, feareth and doth not do the like to them . . . this man shall not die for the iniquity of his father, but living he shall live. Yet you say Why hath not the son borne the iniquity of his father?

[1] Ez 3:17–21. The same warning is repeated 33:2–9

[2] Ez 9:1–11. For another example of individual responsibility and retribution, see Ez 14:1–8

Because the son hath done what is right and just, hath kept all my precepts and done them, living he shall live. The soul that sinneth, the same shall die: the son shall not bear the iniquity of his father and the father shall not bear the iniquity of his son. The righteousness of the righteous shall be upon him, and the wickedness of the wicked shall be upon him'.[1]

The occasion of this emphatic teaching of individual responsibility was a proverb that became current at this time in Israel. 'The word of Yahweh came to me, saying: What mean you that you use this proverb among the children of Israel, The fathers have eaten sour grapes and the teeth of the children are set on edge. As I live, saith the Lord Yahweh, you shall not use this proverb any more in Israel'.[2] The prevalence of the saying is further attested by its quotation in the Book of Jeremias: 'In those days they shall say no more The fathers have eaten sour grapes and the teeth of the children are set on edge. But each one shall die for his own iniquity; every man that eateth sour grapes, his own teeth shall be set on edge'.[3] The occasion for the adoption of this proverb came with the unprecedented calamities that swept over the Hebrews at this time. King Josias was defeated and slain at the battle of Megiddo, 609 B.C.[4] Joachaz, his son and successor, was deposed and exiled by Nechao, the Egyptian Pharaoh, and a fine imposed on the land, 609 B.C.[5] He was succeeded by his brother Joakim, in whose time the land was invaded by Nabuchodonosor and became tributary to Babylonia, 605 B.C.[6] The land was further molested during this reign by incursions of Syrians, Moabites, and Ammonites.[7] Then in the reign of his son and successor Joachin, Nabuchodonosor countered the rebellion begun by Joakim by a second invasion. This time he beleaguered Jerusalem. The outcome was that the Babylonian carried away to his own country all the wealth both of the temple and of the royal treasury together

[1] Ez 18:4–20

[2] Ez 18:1–3. The reading of the Septuagint 'among the children of Israel' is preferable to that of the Hebrew text 'in the land of Israel'.

[3] Jer 31:29f.

[4] 2(4) Kg 23:29

[5] 2(4) Kg 23:33f.

[6] 2(4) Kg 24:1; Dan 1:1

[7] 2(4) Kg 24:2

with the king himself and all the citizens of any importance. 'None were left but the poor sort of the people of the land'.[1] This happened in 598 B.C. Sedecias, the next king, another son of Josias, had the temerity again to throw off the yoke of Babylon.[2] This led to the final siege of Jerusalem and its capture. Nabuchodonosor 'burnt the house of Yahweh and the king's palace and all the houses of Jerusalem'. The land was at the mercy of the invader and the campaign culminated in another great deportation, 587 B.C.[3]

Now already during the reign of Manasses, 698/7–643/2, the prophets had foretold that great evils were to come on the land because of the iniquities of that monarch: 'Yahweh spoke through his servants the prophets, saying: Because Manasses king of Judah hath done these most wicked abominations beyond all that the Amorites did before him and hath made Judah also to sin with his idols'.[4] And again in the reign of Josias, 641/0–609, a similar prophecy had been uttered by Jeremias: 'I will make them a fear-inspiring spectacle for all the kingdoms of the earth, because of Manasses the son of Ezechias, the king of Judah, for all that he did in Jerusalem'.[5] The Israelites of the time seem to have fixed on such pronouncements and concluded that they were being made victims for the wickedness of their fathers. If so, they fixed on the words that suited their plea and overlooked accompanying denunciations. The prophecy quoted from the servants of God who were contemporaries of Manasses, continues: 'Because they have done evil before me and have continued to provoke me from the day that their fathers came out of Egypt even unto this day'.[6] And the prophecy of Jeremias likewise continues with words addressed to Jerusalem: 'Thou hast forsaken me, saith Yahweh, thou art gone backward . . . I am weary of having compassion'.[7] And they persevered in all their wickedness in spite of many warnings through the prophets until the catastrophe broke upon the land. The

[1] 2(4) Kg 24:11–16
[2] 2(4) Kg 24:20
[3] 2(4) Kg 25:1–21
[4] 2(4) Kg 21:10f.
[5] Jer 15:4. See also 2 (4) Kg 23:26–27; 24:3f.
[6] 2(4) Kg 21:15
[7] Jer 15:6

following quotation deals with the state of morals during the reign of Sedecias the last king, 598–587: 'Moreover all the princes of Judah and the priests and the people multiplied their wicked transgressions according to all the abominations of the Gentiles, and they defiled the house of Yahweh which he had sanctified in Jerusalem. And Yahweh, the God of their fathers, sent to them continually through his messengers, because he had pity on his people and his dwelling-place. But they mocked the messengers of God and despised his words and misused the prophets until the wrath of Yahweh rose against his people and there was no remedy'.[1] The chastisement was due to the continued wickedness of the nation persisting despite the preaching of the prophets right up to the destruction of kingdom and capital. The great exile followed, and it happened according to the words of Leviticus: 'they shall pine away for the iniquities of their fathers and their own'.[2]

This leads to the question whether the emphasis laid by Ezechiel on individual responsibility entailed the abolition of corporate responsibility. And this question involves consideration both of the nature of human society in itself and of the treatment of the matter in the text of the Bible. As regards the first of these considerations, it is a fundamental law governing the relations of human beings that they should group themselves in societies. The necessity of such grouping arises from the inescapable interdependence of men on each other. Man is by nature a social being. And the nature of a society involves corporate personality and corporate personality involves corporate responsibility. It is therefore inevitable that the members of a society should be involved in the consequences of the actions of the society to which they belong. They enjoy the advantages of its wise acts (and there is no true wisdom where there is no regard for the moral law) and, on the other hand, they must individually suffer the evil effects of its unwise and wicked acts. Such, then, being the nature of

[1] 2 Par 36:14–16. The opening words are translated here according to the Septuagint (B).

[2] Lev 26:39

man and the inevitable results of his association with his fellows, it cannot have been the intention of the Book of Ezechiel to suggest such a radical transformation of human society as could eliminate corporate personality and corporate responsibility. When innocent members of a corporate body suffer for the evil acts of the body to which they belong, their sufferings are not a punishment, although the same sufferings may be a punishment of the guilty members of the same body. All are involved in the common lot.[1]

A consideration of biblical texts leads to the same conclusion. Ezechiel himself recognises that the law of individual retribution suffers exceptions. In chap. 14 where he insists that in a guilty land doomed by God the presence of men famed for their righteousness will not avail to save even their own sons and daughters, he none the less learns from God that some of the wicked in Jerusalem will be saved and will come to Babylonia as evident proofs by their wickedness of the justice of God's punishment of the city. 'There shall be left in it some that shall be saved, who shall bring away their sons and daughters. Behold they shall come among you, and you shall see their way and their doings; and you shall be comforted concerning the evil that I have brought upon Jerusalem, in all things that I have brought upon it. And they shall comfort you, when you see their ways and their doings; and you shall know that I have not done without cause all that I have done in it, saith the Lord God'.[2] So some escape to manifest God's justice for the benefit of their fellow-countrymen. And conversely it is revealed to him that in the destruction of Jerusalem just persons will suffer with the wicked. 'The word of the Lord came to me, saying: Son of man, set thy face toward Jerusalem . . . and say to the land of Israel: Thus saith the Lord God: Behold I come against thee, and I will draw forth my sword out of its sheath and will cut off in thee just and wicked'.[3]

Jeremias also repudiated the use made by his contemporaries of the proverb about the eating of sour grapes.[4]

[1] See the remarks on this subject, p. 69
[2] Ez 14:22f.
[3] Ez 21:1–3 (HT 21:6–8)
[4] Jer 31:29 f. See p. 91

But he does not repudiate the idea of national responsibility: 'When . . . they shall say to thee: Wherefore hath Yahweh pronounced against us all this great evil? What is our iniquity, and what is our sin that we have sinned against Yahweh our God? Thou shalt say to them because your fathers forsook me, saith Yahweh, and went after strange gods and served them and adored them, and forsook me and kept not my law. And you have done worse than your fathers, for, behold, every one of you walketh after the perverseness of his evil heart, so as not to hearken to me. So I will cast you forth out of this land into a land which neither you nor your fathers have known'.[1] And later he addresses God in words taken from Ex 20:5: 'Thou shewest mercy unto the thousandth generation and requitest the iniquity of the fathers into the bosom of their children after them'. And in this same prayer the prophet's emphasis on individual retribution shows that in his mind there is no conflict between this and his immediately preceding statement: 'Thine eyes are open upon all the ways of the sons of man to render unto each one according to his ways and according to the fruit of his devices'.[2] And in a passage of the Book of Isaias that is increasingly recognised to be later than the work of Ezechiel, we read: 'Behold it is written before me. I will not be silent, but I will render and repay into their bosom your iniquities and the iniquities of your fathers together, saith Yahweh'.[3] Similarly in the Lamentations of Jeremias, which date from after the fall of Jerusalem, the people pray: 'Our fathers have sinned and we have borne their iniquities'.[4] And there has been occasion already in these pages to refer to the words of Christ our Lord that all the just blood that had been shed upon the earth from the blood of Abel to the blood of Zacharias would come upon His generation.[5] This shows that the principle involved was not one of temporary validity which would cease to have effect when the Old Testament was substituted by the New.

The clear teaching of Ezechiel notwithstanding, the idea

[1] Jer 16:10–13
[2] Jer 32:18f. On 'the thousandth generation', see p. 67
[3] Is 65:6f. [4] Lam 5:7 [5] p. 69

long prevailed among the Jews that men are punished for the sins of their parents. The fifth of the seven brothers martyred by Antiochus Epiphanes, 176/5–164/3, thus addressed his tormentor : 'As you have authority among men, you do what you like, mortal though you are, but do not think that our race has been forsaken by God. Wait a while and you will see the greatness of his power and how he will torment you and your seed '.[1] And even in New Testament times we have the record of the question asked by the disciples of our Lord : 'Rabbi, who hath sinned, this man or his parents, that he should be born blind ?' He at once corrected their error : 'Neither hath this man sinned nor his parents, but that the works of God should be made manifest in him '.[2]

The results of our investigation in this chapter may now be briefly summarised. The doctrine of individual responsibility was not new in the sixth century. It goes back to the beginnings of Hebrew history. In early times, however, owing to the Covenant having been made with the people as a whole, considerable prominence was given to corporate, national responsibility. But when the calamitous times preceding the exile and the exile itself brought untold sufferings on all and they tried to excuse themselves with the false plea that they were being punished for the sins of their fathers, the moment was opportune for the doctrine of individual responsibility to be preached with new emphasis. Neither was this new emphasis on the individual a denial of the doctrine of corporate responsibility. We may end with a quotation from H. H. Rowley : 'It is sometimes supposed that Jeremiah and Ezekiel discovered the individual. This is a gross exaggeration. . . . It is not true that hitherto man had been regarded solely as a member of the community. Nor did these two prophets regard him solely as an individual. With them there came a new emphasis on the individual, rather than a discovery of the individual '.[3]

[1] 2 Macc 7:16f.
[2] Jn 9:2f. See the additional note at the end of chap. x
[3] H. H. Rowley, *The Re-Discovery of the Old Testament* (London [1946])

Chapter VII

THE SUFFERING OF THE INNOCENT: VICARIOUS SUFFERING

The theme of the lot due respectively to the good and the bad became enshrined in the sayings of the Book of Proverbs.

> The curse of Yahweh is on the house of the wicked,
> But the habitation of the just is blessed.[1]
> Treasures of wickedness shall profit nothing,
> But righteousness shall deliver from death.
> Yahweh will not afflict the soul of the just with famine,
> But the desires of the wicked he will disappoint.[2]

The principle was thus well known to the people at large, and appeal was wrongly made to it by men who were suffering but by no means innocent, even after Jeremias and Ezechiel had exposed the falseness of the complaint made in their time about the eating of sour grapes. So after the exile, when the condition of the people was miserable and in no way corresponded to the bright hopes they had entertained, they complained of God's justice. Malachy sets this down in his characteristic dialogue form. 'You have wearied Yahweh with your sayings, yet you say "In what have we wearied him?" By your saying "Every one that doth evil is good in the sight of Yahweh and such are pleasing to him; or surely where is the God of judgement?"'[3] And the prophet had to point out to them that the fault was on their side and that they were daring to blame God when the blame was due to their own behaviour. 'From the days of your fathers you have departed from my ordinances and have not kept them'. That was the reason why they were under a curse and why the locusts devoured the fruits of their fields and why their

[1] Prov 3:33 [2] Prov 10:2f. [3] Mal 2:17

vines were barren. But instead of confessing their own faults they had used harsh words against God. 'Yet you say "What have we spoken against thee ?" You have said, "He laboureth in vain that serveth God and what profit is it that we have kept his ordinances and have walked with self-restraint before Yahweh of hosts ?" Wherefore now we call the proud happy ; they are even built up that work wickedness ; they have made trial of God and are preserved '.[1]

Others also, however, who were not themselves guilty, none the less at times felt themselves neglected by God. Thus the prophet Habacuc, whose mission fell in the seventh century sometime before the Babylonian Empire became a menace to Judah :

> How long, O Yahweh, shall I cry out
> And thou wilt not listen ?
> How long shall I call to thee of oppression
> And thou wilt not give deliverance ?
> Why hast thou made me see inquity and perverseness,
> To look upon rapine and injustice ? . . .
> The wicked prevaileth against the just.[2]
>
> Thine eyes are too pure to behold evil
> And thou canst not look on perverseness ;
> Why lookest thou upon the treacherous
> And holdest thy peace while the wicked
> Destroyeth one more just than himself ? [3]

Jeremias too, who had so much to suffer in the cause of his mission, cried out to God :

> Thou art in the right, O Yahweh,
> If I contend with thee ;
> Yet would I utter my pleas before thee !
> Why doth the way of the wicked prosper ?
> Why is it well with them that practise treachery ?

[1] Mal 3:7–15 [2] Hab 1:2–4 [3] Hab 1:13

Thou hast planted them and they have taken root;
  They prosper and bring forth fruit.
Thou art near in their mouths
  But far from their hearts.
And thou, O Yahweh, dost know me and seest me;
  Thou hast tried my heart towards thee.
Drag them away like sheep for slaying;
  Prepare them for the day of slaughter!
How long shall the land mourn
  And all the herbs of the field wither
  For the malice of the dwellers therein?
The beasts and the birds are consumed,
  Because they say 'God doth not see our ways'.[1]

The theme recurs in Ecclesiastes. 'I have seen everything', he says, 'in my days of vanity: it happens that a just man perisheth in his righteousness and that a wicked man liveth long in his wickedness'.[2] But he did not lose his trust. 'I have seen the wicked carried to the grave who had frequented the holy place and were praised in the city as men who had acted rightly. This also is vanity. Because sentence is not speedily executed against evil deeds, therefore the heart of the sons of man is set to do evil. Though a sinner do evil a hundred times and prolong his days, yet I know too that it shall be well with them that reverence God, that have reverence before him, but that well it shall not be for the wicked and that he shall not prolong his days like a shadow because he hath not reverence before God. There is a vanity which occurreth upon the earth, for there are just men to whom it happeneth according to the doing of the wicked, and there are wicked men to whom it happeneth according to the doing of the just. I say that this also is vanity'.[3] That God should so have directed His providence and should have inspired these words to be enshrined in Holy Scripture was certainly for a purpose. And that purpose seems to have been to awaken men to the

[1] Jer 12:1–4. In the last line the Hebrew has 'see our last end', but the Septuagint reading suits the context and is doubtless right. It supposes a Hebrew word almost identical with that in our existing Hebrew text.
[2] Ecclesiastes 7:16 (HT 15) [3] Ecclesiastes 8:10–14

imperfection of their conception of His designs for mankind and gradually to bring them to a realisation that their this-worldly view of His government of the world was wholly incomplete. Their knowledge of God's absolute justice and their growing appreciation of the inequality of retribution in this world worked together to awaken in their souls the conviction that God's retribution for good and evil is not confined to this life but receives its adequate complement after death. One more quotation from Ecclesiastes will help to show how strongly this ferment must have worked in moulding the thoughts and belief of the spiritually minded in a way that would eventually influence the belief of the people at large. 'All things happen equally to the just and to the wicked, to the good and to the evil, to the clean and to the unclean, to him that offereth victims and to him that doth not. As the good, so also is the sinner; as the perjured, so also he that hath reverence for an oath. This is an evil among all things that are done under the sun that the same things happen to all men. Yea also the hearts of the children of men are full of evil, and folly is in their hearts while they live, and in the end they join the dead '.[1] These words, it must be emphasised, are not just the human reflections of a Jewish thinker but reflections which God Almighty through inspiration wished to be communicated in the first instance to the Jewish people and to find a place in their Canon of Sacred Scripture. There is consequently nothing in them of unauthorised or indiscreet criticism. They were inspired for a purpose, which seems to have been, as suggested, to raise the minds of the chosen people to higher thoughts of God's manner of apportioning rewards and punishments.

From these thoughts we may turn to the suffering that could be brought on a servant of God in the course of and on account of his mission. Of such sorrow, afflictions, and even persecution the prophet Jeremias is an outstanding example.

[1] Ecclesiastes 9:2f. The Douay Version translates ' the same things happen to all men ; whereby also the hearts of the children of men are filled with evil ', thereby establishing a connection between the prevalence of evil and the apparent lack of discriminating retribution. This is not explicit in the text but probably renders the thought correctly.

He felt himself at times heart-broken by the sufferings that it was his duty to announce as punishment for the sins of his people.

For the affliction of the daughter of my people I am afflicted;
 I am sad; desolation hath seized upon me.
Is there no balm in Galaad?
 Is there no healer there?
Why is not the wound
 Of the daughter of my people healed?
Who will give water to my head
 And a fountain of tears to my eyes
And I will weep day and night
 For the slain of the daughter of my people.[1]
For the mountains I will raise my voice in weeping and lamentation,
 And for the pastures of the wilderness in a song of mourning.
Because they are burnt up and no man passeth through
 And they hear not the voice of the flock.
From the birds of the sky and to the beasts
 They are fled away, they are departed.[2]
I was as a meek lamb
 That is led to the slaughter.
And I knew that they had devised counsels against me:
 'Let us destroy the tree with its sap
And let us cut him off from the land of the living,
 And let his name be remembered no more'.[3]

His fellow-citizens of Anathoth carried their opposition to his mission to the extent that they openly threatened him with death: 'Prophesy no more in the name of Yahweh and thou shalt not die at our hands'.[4] Such was the anguish Jeremias had to endure that he even broke into laments for the day of his birth.

[1] Jer 8:21–9:1 (HT 8:21–3). 'The daughter of my people' is a poetic Hebrew expression signifying the whole population.
[2] Jer 9:10 (HT 9) [3] Jer 11:19 [4] Jer 11:21

Woe is me, my mother, that thou didst bear me
A man of strife and contention to all the earth !
I am no man's creditor and no man's debtor ;
Yet every man doth curse me.[1]
Why is my sorrow perpetual
And my wound desperate refusing to be healed ? [2]

These sufferings of the great prophet were endured by him in the course of his mission. It was precisely because he was doing his utmost to serve his people that affliction and persecution came upon him. He suffered therefore in the cause of his people, but that is not to say that his sufferings were vicarious. He was not a victim in place of his people.[3] All the misfortunes which he foretold came in fact upon the nation, culminating in the destruction of the holy city and the Babylonian exile. And so far was Jeremias from any idea that he was suffering in place of his people that he prayed God to take vengeance on his persecutors. Such prayers are incompatible with the consciousness of enduring vicarious suffering. They are not prayers for vengeance simply to satisfy personal animosity but prayers that God will visit wicked conduct with just retribution.

Yahweh of hosts, who judgest justly
And triest the reins and the heart,
Let me see thy vengeance upon them,
For to thee have I laid open my cause.[4]

They say, 'Come let us invent devices against Jeremias,
For the law shall not perish from the priest,
Nor counsel from the wise nor the word from the prophet'.
Give heed to me, O Yahweh,
And hear the voice of mine adversaries !

[1] Jer 15:10 [2] Jer 15:18

[3] O. Eissfeldt, the distinguished professor of Halle, has expressed a contrary opinion : 'Jeremiah seems to have been conscious that he must suffer want and pain not only innocently but also vicariously', ET 44 (1932/3) 265*b*. The passages to which he appeals are 15:10, 15*b*, 18 ; 16:1–2 ; 18:20

[4] Jer 11:20

Shall evil be rendered for good,
  Because they have dug a pit for my life?
Remember that I have stood in thy sight
  To speak good for them
  And to turn away thy wrath from them!
Therefore deliver up their children to famine
  And hand them over to the power of the sword![1]

In this passage the prophet stresses that his sufferings have come upon him in spite of his intercession for the people and his efforts for their good—indeed, not merely in spite of them but precisely because of them. Elsewhere he says in so many words that his sufferings are due to his work for God's cause: 'Know that for thy sake I have suffered reproach'.[2]

In the story of Jeremias's mission, then, we have the case of a prophet suffering in the cause of his people but not precisely in their stead.[3] His sufferings were not offered or accepted by God as a substitute for the punishment due to the sins of the nation for which he laboured. A closer approach to vicarious suffering is found in the history of the Maccabees. The seven brothers martyred by Antiochus Epiphanes did not suffer as substitutes for their nation, but they offered up their martyrdom for its good. This goes beyond the use of intercessory prayer for others, of which there are examples from the earliest times in Hebrew history.[4] It is a recognition of the meritorious value of suffering undergone for God's cause and an offering to God of that merit for the benefit of others. The seventh of the brothers addressed the tyrant as follows: 'I, like my brothers, give up both body and life for the laws of our fathers, calling on God speedily to be gracious to our nation and to bring you amid afflictions and tortures to confess that he only is God, and through me and my brothers to stay

[1] Jer 18:18–21 [2] Jer 15:15

[3] Similarly the psalmist speaking in the person of the nation, 43(44):23:

Nay, for thy sake are we slain all the day,
  Are we reckoned as sheep for the slaughter.

According to Hebrew idiom the phrase 'for thy sake' must be understood also with the second half of the verse. See also Ps 68(69):8

[4] Gen 18:23–32; 20:7; Num 16:20–4; Job 42:8–10

the wrath of the Almighty which has justly fallen on all our race'.[1] This is a very noble speech. It accepts suffering willingly and without repine, recognises that suffering so borne for religion has a value in the eyes of God, and offers it up for the benefit of others. This brings the seven Maccabean martyrs very close to the suffering Servant of Yahweh, to whom we must now turn.

For a full appreciation of the passages about the mission of the Servant and its outcome they must be read carefully in their context. The strange idea that they have been inserted here and there in the Book of Isaias without regard to the context, has been proposed, but apart from the psychological improbability of such a proceeding, especially concerning a theme of outstanding importance, against such a suggestion stands the difficulty experienced in the attempt to delimit these passages. The gravity of this difficulty is manifested by the variety of the solutions offered, and the difficulty indicates not independence of but connection with the context. However, for the purpose of the present study all that is required is an outline of the Servant's mission with special attention to its outcome.

The Servant is one whom the Lord has chosen and in whom He takes delight. He has received the spirit of God to fit him for his mission, which is to make known the way of justice and righteousness to the Gentiles. His method will not be that of violence and conquest by war. On the contrary, it will be gentleness itself.

> The bruised reed he shall not break,
> And the glimmering wick he shall not quench.

He will persevere with his task till he establishes righteousness in the earth. The islands, the distant regions, await his teaching, not indeed consciously but because at heart they are aware of the imperfection of their religious beliefs. God destines the Servant to establish a covenant with His people and to be a light to the Gentiles—

[1] 2 Macc 7:37f. Cp. 4 Macc 6:28f.; 17:21f.

To open the eyes of the blind
And to bring forth the captive out of prison
And those that sit in darkness out of confinement.[1]

Despite his call and mission from God and the divine help accorded him the Servant feels his labours to be in vain.

This was my thought: I have laboured in vain;
For nought and to no effect have I spent my strength.

Again the mission of the Servant is announced:

It is too light a thing for thee to be my servant
To raise up the tribes of Jacob
And to bring back those preserved of Israel.
I have set thee to be the light of the Gentiles,
To be my salvation to the ends of the earth.

Such are the words of Yahweh, the Holy One of Israel to 'the soul that is despised, to him that is abhorred of the nation'.

Kings shall see and shall arise,
Princes, and they shall adore.

And again it is said that the Servant is to establish a covenant with the people. His mission is a double one, both to Israel and to the nations.[2]

But in the course of his mission the Servant was to endure more than discouragement and lack of success.

The Lord Yahweh hath opened my ear,
And I do not resist;
I have not gone back.
I have given my back to the smiters
And my cheeks to those that plucked them.
My face I have not hid
From insults and spittle.

[1] Is 42:1–7 [2] Is 49:1–8

But conscious of his call and of divine help nothing could deter the Servant from the prosecution of his mission.

> I have set my face as a flint;
> And I know that I shall not be confounded.[1]

In spite of all opposition and persecution the Servant is confident that with God's help his mission will not in the end be a failure.

On the contrary his end will be glorious and will excite the wonder of kings. But his path to final glory will be the hard path of martyrdom, of death suffered for the sins of men.

> Lo, my servant shall prosper[2];
> He shall be exalted and shall be raised exceeding high . . .

Kings will be silent in wonder—

> For they shall see what had not been told them,
> And shall behold what they had not heard.

It would all have seemed incredible, so lowly and humble were his beginnings.

> There was no comeliness in him and no majesty that we should look upon him,
> And no beauty that we should be desirous of him.
> Despised and the most abject of men,
> A man of sorrows and acquainted with infirmity;
> Like one from whom men avert their gaze,
> Despised and we esteemed him not.
> But our infirmities it was he bore
> And our sorrows were his burden.
> Yet we esteemed him smitten,
> Stricken by God and afflicted;
> Whereas he was wounded for our transgressions
> And crushed for our iniquities.

[1] Is 50:1–7 [2] Is 52:13

Chastisement to give us peace was upon him
And by his weals we are healed.
All we like sheep had gone astray;
We had turned aside each to his own way.
But Yahweh laid upon him
The iniquity of us all.
He was oppressed but humbled himself
And opened not his mouth.
He was led like a sheep to the slaughter
And like a ewe before its shearers
He was dumb and opened not his mouth.
From confinement and sentence he was taken off;
And who gave thought to his lot?[1]
That he was cut off from the land of the living;
That he was stricken for the transgression of my people.
They assigned his grave with the wicked;
And in death they put him with the rich,
Although he had done no violence
And there was no deceit in his mouth.
But Yahweh who had willed to crush him,
Restored him who gave his life a sin-offering.[2]
He shall see a long-lived seed,
And the will of Yahweh shall prosper in his hand.

Then the theme of the Servant's vicarious suffering and its atoning power recurs.

My servant shall make many righteous,
And their iniquities he shall bear.

His reward will be very great—

For that he poured out his soul to death
And was numbered with transgressors.
Yet he bore the sin of many
And maketh intercession for transgressors.[3]

[1] For the meaning 'lot, fate' assigned to *dôr*, see G. R. Driver in JTS 36 (1935) 403. [2] This emendation and translation is based in part on J. Ziegler's edition of Isaias in the Echter Bibel. [3] Is 52:13–53:12.

In this poem is reached the climax of Old Testament teaching on the value of suffering. It is seen that willingly borne it has atoning value and is accepted by God in satisfaction for sin. And not only may a man atone for his own wickedness but his sufferings avail before God also for the pardon of others. In the poem the death of the Suffering Servant is said to avail for 'many', but it must be noticed that according to Hebrew idiom this word does not exclude the idea of universality. All are many, and the latter word seems to have been used by Hebrew writers to emphasise the idea of the multitude of those envisaged. In other words 'many' is not meant in an exclusive sense and may be legitimately interpreted to embrace all. The story of the New Testament reveals the identity of the Servant about whom this great prophecy was uttered. Christ our Lord was, as holy Simeon declared in his prayer to God, 'a light to the revelation of the Gentiles and the glory of thy people Israel'.[1] He came 'to give his life a redemption for many', as He Himself declared.[2] He entered into a new Covenant and shed His Blood for the atonement of sin: 'This is my blood of the New Testament which shall be shed for many unto the remission of sins'.[3] And, again according to His own testimony, in Him was fulfilled the saying 'And with the wicked was he reckoned'.[4] This is twice touched on in the poem. Once in so many words 'He was numbered with transgressors' and once in reference to His grave 'They assigned his grave with the wicked'. The line in parallelism with this last 'In death they put him with the rich' provides another instance of that Old Testament usage in which 'rich' and 'wicked' are practically synonymous terms.[5] The closing sentence that the Servant makes 'intercession for transgressors' are echoed in the Epistle to the Hebrews: 'He is able also to save for

[1] Lk 2:32
[2] Mt 20:28
[3] Mt 26:28
[4] Lk 22:37
[5] Cp. p. 78. The word 'rich' is attested in the LXX, Vulgate, and Peshitta, and in view of Old Testament usage there is no reason to alter it. That our Lord was buried in the sepulchre of Joseph of Arimathea does not invalidate the prophecy, the leading idea of which is not to foretell exactly the character of His burial-place but His condemnation as a guilty man.

ever them that come to God by him, always living to make intercession for us' ('them').[1]

The texts studied in this chapter on the suffering of the innocent have revealed a progressive understanding of God's ways with man. The original idea that sin is punished by misfortune and suffering, though true in itself, tended to make men think that the converse is also true and that suffering is always a sign of foregoing guilt. Hence men who suffered without consciousness of guilt were apt to be puzzled and complain. It happened, however, not infrequently that men were so inured to evil-doing as to have their consciences seared and to lose the sense of guilt, proclaiming themselves to be innocent sufferers when in fact they were laden with a burden of sin. Jeremias, himself an innocent sufferer, came to realise that his mission involved persecution and suffering and that what he endured, he endured for the sake of God, whose cause he had at heart and strove to promote. But there is no suggestion of vicarious suffering in his career. This was reserved for the prophecy of the suffering and death of the Servant of God whose mission was both to Israel and to the nations, a prophecy fulfilled in Christ our Lord.

[1] Heb 7:25. The Vulgate has 'for us', the Greek 'for them', but the difference is formal only, as all who come to God do so through the grace of Christ.

Chapter VIII

THE SUFFERING OF THE INNOCENT: THE BOOK OF JOB

If the development of doctrine in the Old Testament always proceeded in rectilinear fashion, we should have a further aid to our scanty means of dating its various writings. And, conversely, if we knew in every case the dates at which the books were composed, we should be better able to judge the chronological development of ideas. As it happens, the Book of Job is one in which certain indications of date are lacking and the opinions of authors vary widely. Pfeiffer writes: 'the only conclusion which may be regarded as generally accepted is that the poet lived between 700 and 200 B.C.'.[1] The evidence suggests a date after the destruction of Jerusalem in 587 B.C. but not long after the return of the exiles in 538.[2] The relation, if any, between the Book of Job and the Servant Songs considered in the last chapter has also been differently assessed. Some have considered Job to be chronologically earlier and to have exercised an influence on the theology of the Suffering Servant. So R. H. Pfeiffer. A. Kuenen thought he could discern evidence of the reverse dependence. The internal evidence of the texts, supported by this conflicting appraisal of the situation, rather suggests that that the two were written in complete independence without influence in either direction.[3] The question of the unity of the book and

[1] R. H. Pfeiffer, *Introduction to the Old Testament* (New York 1948) 676. On pp. 676–8 he gives with references an exhaustive list of the dates proposed by different writers.

[2] For further detail, see CC §318*r*. This date agrees in general with that favoured by Pfeiffer, p. 677, 'the time of Jeremiah (or more exactly the period 608–580)', an opinion shared by E. König, N. Schlögl, and others, as Pfeiffer there notes.

[3] R. H. Pfeiffer, *Introd. to the Old Testament* (New York 1948) 677. A. B. Davidson, *The Book of Job* (Cambridge 1903 ; The Cambridge Bible for Schools and Colleges) pp. lxvi f. favours the mutual independence of the

what parts show signs of being later additions to the original work[1] need not detain us here. It is a literary problem, which does not affect the chronological development of the theological doctrine as it is presented in the book.

The prose prologue gives the reader the information necessary for the understanding of the subsequent poetic dialogue between Job and his three friends. One of the heavenly court seems to have had the function, not of tempting men to sin, but of testing the reality of their virtue. He is called 'the Satan' or 'the Opponent', a name which later came to be applied as a proper name without the article to the chief of the evil spirits who hate human kind and try to draw them into sin. The Satan, then, declared one day to God Almighty that Job's virtue was merely superficial and was nothing but his response to his wealth and general prosperity. His happy estate being regarded by him as the reward of a good life, he found it worth his while to avoid evil and to do good. But, the Satan continued, if only he were deprived of his wealth and were struck by the hand of adversity, his piety would disappear and he would even break out into blasphemies against God. The Satan thereupon received permission to afflict Job with the sole restriction that he was to spare his life. The holy man is now overwhelmed by calamity. Sudden death snatches away his sons and daughters; his herds and flocks are destroyed by lightning or driven off by marauders; he himself is smitten with a grievous and loathsome disease. The reader is thus put in possession of a knowledge of the true situation. Job is a religious and innocent man. He has done nothing to deserve punishment or to bring these appalling calamities on himself. They are allowed merely as a test of

[1] Some discussion of this matter may be found, for instance, in CC §317*i–p*

two writers: 'These similarities of phraseology might be due to dependence of the one writer upon the other . . . [But] the more probable explanation is that they lived surrounded by the same atmosphere of thought. . . . The author of the one picture might have transferred some features from the canvas of his predecessor to his own. The probability is as great that the two authors worked up common conceptions into independent creations'. And in a note he adds: 'It is difficult to believe that the solution of the problem of suffering innocence given in Job could be posterior to the more profound solution found in the prophet'. Both writers refer to the opinion of Kuenen.

his virtue. Under such crushing blows will he persevere in his good way of life or will he say there is no use in serving God and give up his religion ? But Job himself knows nothing of what passed in heaven, nothing of the reason for his trials. Neither do his friends who hear of his misfortunes and come to console him.

It might be thought that with this straightforward narrative as a guide there could be no doubt as to the purpose of the book and that all writers would be unanimous in its explanation. However, such is not the case. Otto Procksch in his massive volume on the theology of the Old Testament rejects the view that the theme of the book is the meaning of suffering, though he admits that many have understood it to be such and that the book itself appears to warrant the view. And the reason for his rejection is that no answer is given anywhere in the book to the question as to the meaning of suffering, and such an answer would, he holds, have been imperative, had such been in fact the theme of the book. The negative answer, which the book does give, namely that suffering is not a sign of guilt, he holds to be insufficient, and points out that a positive explanation is nowhere proposed. He therefore maintains that the theme of the whole is the justice of God. To this it may be answered that neither does the book contain any positive solution of the question how God's justice is to be reconciled with Job's suffering. Moreover, the question as to God's justice is never formally proposed. Job in the extremity of his misery and in his inability to understand why he should be so afflicted does complain that he has been deprived of his right, 27:2. But this is only a passing mood ; in his heart of hearts he knows that his complaint is not justified. At other times he appeals to the justice of God. So overwrought is he by his prolonged misery and by the unsympathetie attitude of his friends that he appeals to the tribunal of God the just judge against the same God whom he feels to be persecuting him.

O that I could find him !
I would go to his abode.

I would set forth my case before him
  And would fill my mouth with pleas.
I would know with what words he would answer me,
  And I would understand what he would say to me.
Would he strive against me with massive strength?
  No! Most surely he would give me hearing.
There a just man could reason with him;
  And I should be free for ever from my judge.[1]

The justice of God is never seriously in question, and no formal defence of it is offered. So the argument used by Procksch to reject suffering as the theme uppermost in the author's mind is fatal against his own proposed interpretation. Moreover, the justice of God was a belief so fundamental in the religion of the Hebrews that it would not suggest itself to them as a theme to be debated.

The debate between Job and his friends is consistently confined to the question what is the cause of his calamities. The so-called comforters hold to the belief that misfortune is a sign and proof of guilt, a belief which they have deduced from the converse proposition that guilt is punished by calamity. At first they give only gentle hints of their conviction, being unwilling to accuse Job openly of iniquity.

Remember now, what innocent man ever perished?
  And where have the upright been destroyed?
Even as I have seen, the ploughers of iniquity
  And the sowers of harm do reap the same.
By the breath of God they perish
  And by the blast of his wrath they are consumed.[2]

So Eliphaz in his first speech. Bildad in his opening talk suggests that Job's children died on account of their wrongdoing.

If thy children sinned against him
  And he delivered them over to the power of their transgression,

[1] Job 23:3–7 [2] Job 4:7–9

If thou dost seek God diligently
And implore the mercy of the Omnipotent,
If thou art pure and upright,
Surely now he will hear thy intercession
And will restore thy habitation in righteousness.[1]

As the dialogue develops the accusations become more open. Thus Eliphaz addresses the sufferer harshly—

Thine iniquity instructeth thy mouth
And thou choosest the tongue of the crafty.
Thy own mouth doth condemn thee and not I,
And thy lips bear witness against thee.[2]

And again—

Behold, in his Holy Ones he doth not trust,
And the heavens are not pure in his eyes.
How much more a man abominable and corrupt,
That drinketh wickedness like water.[3]

One more quotation from Eliphaz will make manifest the judgment the friends had formed of Job and that without other evidence than that of his sufferings. To their thinking no other explanation was possible except that his appearance of virtue was all deception and that he had in fact been guilty of great, though secret, sins.

Is it because thou art religious that he rebuketh thee
And entereth into judgment with thee?
Is not thine evil great?
And are not thine iniquities without limit?
For thou takest pledges of thy brethren without cause,
And tearest off the clothing of the naked.
Water to the weary thou dost not give,
And from the hungry thou withholdest bread.[4]

[1] Job 8:4–6
[2] Job 15:5f.
[3] Job 15:15f.
[4] Job 22:4–7

But in spite of all the insistence of his friends and in face of all their arguments drawn from their own experience and from the tradition of their forefathers Job remains constant in his assertion of his innocence. He has done nothing to merit the calamities that overwhelm him. He does not claim to be entirely blameless.

> Why dost thou not forgive my transgression
>   And take away mine iniquity?[1]
> Thou writest against me deeds of the past,
>   And restorest to me the iniquities of my youth.[2]

But he can never admit the wickedness of which the friends accuse him nor any wickedness which could account for his sufferings as condign punishment.

> Behold now, I have set out my case;
>   I know that right is on my side.[3]
> My face is red with weeping
>   And darkness is on my eyelids,
> Though there is no violence in my hands
>   And my prayer is pure.
> O earth, hide not my blood
>   And let no place hold back my cry!
> Even now my witness is in heaven
>   And my attestor is on high.[4]

And Job's final speech contains a solemn asseveration of his abstention from evil. It manifests a lofty conception of man's moral obligations. The opening lines are as follows:

> I have made a covenant with my eyes
>   Not to look upon a maid,
> For what would be my portion from God above
>   Or what my inheritance from the Almighty in the heights . . .

[1] Job 7:21 [2] Job 13:26
[3] Job 13:18 [4] Job 16:17–20 (HT 16–19)

If I have walked in vanity
  And my foot hath hasted to deceit,
Let him weigh me in a just balance,
  And God will know my integrity.
If my steps have turned out of the way,
  And my heart hath gone after my eyes,
  And aught hath cleaved to my hands,
May I sow and another eat
  And let my crops be rooted out.[1]

Here the debate ends. After this noble speech of the sufferer the friends are silent. To the end they have maintained his guilt and he his innocence. With all the eloquence of the disputants the theological aspect of the problem is not advanced, but the poet has made his point. He leaves the reader convinced that suffering is not a proof of guilt and that God does allow the virtue of the just man to be most severely tested. The corrective value of suffering is briefly touched on by Eliphaz, but this, of course, supposes the guilt of the sufferer.

Blessed is the man whom God correcteth.
  And do not thou reject the chastising of the Almighty !
For he inflicteth pain but bindeth up ;
  He striketh but his hands do heal.[2]

This point is elaborated at length by Elihu,[3] the young man who takes it on himself to continue the argument against Job and to supplement the reasons of the friends which he found pitifully lacking in cogency. But though his speech is long, he does not in fact advance the debate, and he receives no answer from Job nor is reference made to him in the rest of the book.

After Elihu's discourse had ended, God Himself deigned to show Himself. This theophany answered Job's confident assertion not only of his own innocence but of his conviction that even on this earth and before his death God would publicly espouse his cause and manifest the rightfulness of his pleading.

[1] Job 31:1–8 [2] Job 5:17f. [3] Job 33:19–30

I know that my redeemer liveth
And that my warrant will stand upon the earth.
Should my skin be torn from my flesh,
Even after this I shall see God,
Whom I shall see and mine eyes shall behold.[1]

It might have been expected that God Almighty would now reveal to Job what has all along been known to the reader and acquaint him with the fact that the purpose of his calamities was only to test the sincerity of his virtue and in no way reflected on the innocence of his conduct. But no word is said on this subject. Mere men are not to expect to know the secrets of God's government of the world. Not only is their status in the universe as mortal creatures too lowly to warrant participation in God's high counsels, but they are in every way too ignorant and their intellects too feeble for them even to be able to comprehend God's designs. Man must humbly confess his own incapacity and acknowledge the omnipotence, omniscience, and wisdom of the Creator of the world. This lesson is driven home in crushing demonstration couched in language of striking poetic beauty. 'The first speech of Jehovah transcends all other descriptions of the wonders of creation or the greatness of the Creator, which are to be found either in the Bible or elsewhere'.[2] In a convincing proof of his ignorance and impotence Job is led to understand the truth and at the same time the true import of his own words.

What is man that thou dost set store by him
And dost fix thy thoughts upon him?[3]

[1] Job 19:25–7. For the restoration of the order of the words in 26, see *Biblica* 31 (1950) 377f. The passage cannot refer to a future life after death. Had this been Job's thought the whole course of the discussion would have taken a different turn. In fact it proceeds after this declaration on precisely the same lines as before. For a fuller discussion of this point the reader may be referred to Sutcliffe, *Future Life*, 131–7.

[2] S. R. Driver, *Introduction to the Literature of the Old Testament* (Edinburgh 1929⁹) 427

[3] Job 7:17

Man comes and goes in a world created by God at a time when man was nothing.

> Where wast thou when I laid the foundations of the earth ?
> Tell me, if thou hast knowledge and understanding.
> Who laid down the measures thereof if thou knowest,
> Or who stretched out the line upon it ?
> On what were its foundations grounded ?
> Or who laid the corner-stone thereof ?
> When the morning stars sang together
> And all the sons of God made joyful melody ? [1]

All the forces of nature are in the control of God. They require His power and His wisdom for their harmonious working. What control has man over the dawn ? What power has he to make the earth quake ? The stars in their courses do not obey the voice of man and the lightning does not wait for his command. Even the animal creation, over which dominion has been given to man, is largely beyond his control and is full of mysteries.

> Dost thou know what time the mountain goats bring forth ?
> Hast thou observed the hinds when they fawn ? [2]
> Doth the hawk soar through thy wisdom
> Spreading his wings to the south ? [3]

All proves the power of God and the helplessness of man. All proves the wisdom of God and the ignorance of man. The lesson is clear and it is left to Job to take it to heart. If man is so impotent and so ignorant in regard to the world of things that he can see and touch, how can he imagine himself fit to sit in judgment on God's moral government of the universe. Here the issues are far more complex and far more difficult to understand. The only course for man is humbly to acknowledge his own incompetence, to put absolute trust in God knowing that His dispositions, whatever they may be, are wise and just and good. Job's 'suffering is as mysterious

[1] Job 38:4–7 [2] Job 39:1 [3] Job 39:26

as ever, but plain or mysterious, why should it vex him any longer? He has seen God and has entered into rest. . . . [Once] we know God we can trust Him to the uttermost; we know, incredible though it may seem, that the world's misery does not contradict the love of God '.[1]

So Job submits unreservedly and confesses that he admits his folly.

> I know that thou canst do all things
> And that nothing is impossible to thee.
> Therefore have I spoken but not with understanding,
> Of marvels beyond me which I knew not.[2]

God thereupon rewarded the sufferer and 'blessed the latter end of Job more than his beginning'. He is again blessed with a numerous family of seven sons and three daughters, and his flocks and herds are twice as numerous as before. He lives to a ripe old age and sees his children's children to the fourth generation.

Thus the Book of Job both transcends the older Old Testament conception of suffering and yet remains within it. It transcends it in that it definitely teaches that suffering may in God's providence fall on a good man to test the reality of his virtue. Virtue is not necessarily co-extensive with prosperity; calamity is no sure sign of misdeeds. The book yet remains within the purview of the Old Testament in that the story ends and, given the stage of revelation reached at the time of its composition, could not but end in the renewed prosperity of the sufferer. Without the epilogue the poem would be a torso. The epilogue conveys the lesson, though in an incomplete form, that continued suffering for the just is no part of God's plan. Whatever they may have to endure and endure in the right spirit will in God's good time be met with a great reward. A subsidiary lesson is also taught that suffering and calamity have a medicinal or correctional value, which will be more or less efficacious according as the afflicted person re-acts to his trial.

[1] Peake, *Problem*, 88 [2] Job 42:2f.

Chapter IX

SUFFERING IN THE LIGHT OF THE FUTURE LIFE

When the providence of God finally brought the Jewish people as a whole to the belief in a future life where happiness awaited the good and punishment the evil, their thoughts concerning suffering and afflictions underwent a profound change. The belief was slow in maturing and does not seem to have been widely held till perhaps some time in the third pre-Christian century. In the second century it was the prevalent view as shown in the history of the Maccabees and it is taken for granted in the later Book of Wisdom. But though it became the accepted belief of the Pharisees and the people at large, who followed their teaching, it was never accepted by the whole nation. Still in New Testament times the Sadducees rejected the idea of the resurrection and denied the existence both of Angels and of the human spirit.[1]

The new light in which torments and death were viewed by those who believed in a happy immortality is manifest in the brave answers of the Maccabean martyrs. They willingly and cheerfully gave up this present life in the certain hope of resurrection to eternal life. Thus the second brother expressed his faith in the following words: 'Thou indeed, O most wicked man, destroyest us out of this present life; but the King of the world will raise up us who die for his laws, to a new and eternal life'.[2] Similarly the third brother: 'When he was required, he quickly put forth his tongue and courageously stretched out his hands and said nobly: "These I have from heaven, but for the laws of God I now despise them, because I hope to receive them again from him". So that the king and his attendants marvelled at the young man's courage,

[1] Acts 23:8; Mt 22:23. Josephus also has it on record that the Sadducees held that the soul perishes with the body, *Antiquitates Judaicae* XVIII i 4.
[2] 2 Macc 7:9

because he esteemed the torments as nothing '.[1] The sixth brother answered with equal bravery and resignation, accepting death as the merited requital for sin : 'Be not greatly deceived ; for we suffer thus for our own doings, having sinned against our God ; marvellous things are come to pass. But do not think that thou shalt escape unpunished, for that thou hast attempted to fight against God '.[2] So too the youngest brother accepted death as deserved for sin : 'We suffer for our own sins. . . . Our brethren, having now endured for a brief space pain that leads to eternal life, have fallen (in death) under God's covenant '.[3] Their glorious mother encouraged all her sons to die for their religion and saw the torments inflicted on them all. She too made her confession of faith and the last of the noble band of martyrs gave back her soul to God. The sacred writer has preserved her words of exhortation : 'The Creator of the world, who fashioned man in his birth and devised the origin of all, he in his mercy will restore to you again both breath and life, as you now despise yourselves for his laws '. And to the youngest son she said : 'Accept death that in the mercy (of God) I may receive thee again with thy brethren '.[4] These sentiments, common to the family of martyrs, mark a new era in the history of religion. Nothing like them is to be found in the earlier pages of the Old Testament. In its earlier phases the religion there set forth had been this-worldly with hardly a thought extending beyond the grave. Here in the history of the Maccabees the emphasis is reversed. No longer is this life the be-all and almost the end-all. Now this life recedes into the background as passing and ephemeral, as only preparation for the true life, that follows death and is God's eternal reward for the virtuous.

This new outlook on life has left its imprint deeply marked in the Book of Wisdom.

The souls of the just are in the hand of God,
And torment shall not touch them.

[1] 2 Macc 7:10–12 [2] 2 Macc 7:18f.
[3] 2 Macc 7:32, 36 [4] 2 Macc 7:23, 29

In the eyes of the foolish they seemed to be dead,
  And their departure was reckoned as calamity,
  And their journey from us destruction ;
But they are in peace.
For if in the sight of men they suffered torment,
  Their hope was full of immortality.
Afflicted a little they shall be much and well rewarded,
  For God made trial of them
  And found them worthy of himself.[1]

In the older view an early death was reckoned a calamity. A man was thought to be cut off in the midst of his days. And a long life was considered, as in the case of Job, to be part of the fitting reward of virtue. That view now gives way to the new outlook on human life.

If the just man come to an early end,
  He shall be at rest.
For venerable old age is not reckoned by time,
  Nor measured by number of years.
But wisdom is men's grey hairs
  And a spotless life is ripe old age.[2]

Then in general terms but with the thought of Enoch's translation as inspiration the text proceeds :

He pleased God and was beloved,
  And living among sinners he was translated.
He was taken away lest wickedness should alter his understanding
  Or deceit beguile his soul. . . .[3]

The line translated just above with the words ' If the just man come to an early end, he shall be at rest ' is found as follows in RV : ' But a righteous man, though he die before his time, shall be at rest '. And DV gives ' But the just man, if he be prevented with death, shall be in rest '.[4] The use of

[1] Wis 3:1–5 [2] Wis 4:7–9 [3] Wis 4:10f.

[4] The word ' prevented ' is used here in a sense derived from the basic meaning of ' to come before ' and so ' to anticipate ' and is equivalent to ' be overtaken by an early death '.

the word ' death ' in these two versions at first sight seems quite natural and beyond criticism, for what is death but the end of life? None the less this use of the word is not true to the spirit of the Book of Wisdom. Its author does not consider the end of the temporal life of the just to be death. He protests against the opinion the wicked formed of the departed just: ' In the eyes of the foolish they seemed to be dead ', 3:2. Accordingly he does not use the word θάνατος ' death ' of the just but τελευτή ' end '; ' they shall see the end of the wise man ', 4:17 (DV and similarly RV). Even the wicked use this same word after their own death when they come to see their own folly and the happiness of the just: ' We fools accounted . . . his end without honour ', 5:4 (RV and similarly DV). This is a subtle point in the use of language and illustrates how carefully the writer chose his words. While still in the heyday of life the wicked had spoken differently of the just: ' Let us condemn him to a shameful death ', 2:20. It is in accordance with this outlook on the state of the just after the separation of soul and body that in the line quoted at the beginning of this paragraph the word used is not the ordinary word for ' to die ' (θνήσκειν, ἀποθνήσκειν) but that derived from τελευτή ' end ', namely τελευτάω 'to come to the end (of life) '. This consideration shows that the true reading in 4:16 is καμών, the word attested by the Codex Sinaiticus and the first hand of the Codex Vaticanus. This word, which means ' one who has finished his labours ' or perhaps ' one outworn ' is used already by Homer as a synonym of the dead. This rarer expression has been changed in the Codex Alexandrinus and by a later hand in the Codex Vaticanus to θανών, a participle of the common verb for ' to die '. The line may be translated: ' The just man, whose toil is over, shall condemn the impious still in life '. Some such version is required in order to be true to the author's mind and choice of words.[1]

[1] In other contexts there would be no objection to the translation ' that is dead ' of DV, RV, and Holmes in R. H. Charles, *The Apocrypha and Pseudepigrapha of the Old Testament* I (Oxford 1913). By some oversight there is no mention of the variant reading in this work.

The teaching of the Book of Wisdom is thus that the just do not die. They pass from one state of life to another which will know no end.

The just live for ever,
  And their reward is with the Lord
  And the care of them with the Most High.
Therefore shall they receive the crown of glory
  And the beauteous diadem from the hand of the Lord.[1]

But whereas the just enjoy the privilege of eternal life, the part of the wicked is perpetual death. Death originated in the malice of the devil and belongs properly to those who are his.

By the envy of the devil death came into the world,
  And the members of his faction do experience it.[2]

And again :

God made not death,
  Neither hath he pleasure in the destruction of the living ;
For he created all things that they might be,
  And the products of the world are life-giving
And there is no poison of destruction in them,
  Neither hath Hades dominion on earth ;
  For righteousness is immortal.
But the impious by their works and words have invited it.[3]
  They deemed it a friend and wasted away.
They made a covenant with it,
  Because they are worthy to be of its faction.[4]

Thus for those who give themselves to the works of the devil the end of life is a true death. For them it is not merely a passage to another and better life. It is the first stage of a continued death, which St John in the Apocalypse was later to call ‘ the second death ’.[5] This continued death is not con-

[1] Wis 5:16f. [2] Wis 2:24
[3] That is, death, resumed from the first line quoted
[4] Wis 1:13–16 [5] Apoc 20:6, 14 ; 21:8

ceived by the author of the Book of Wisdom as a cessation of existence or as denoting loss of consciousness. He describes at length the bitter recognition of their blindness and folly that will come home to the impious in the next world.

> Then shall the just man stand with great constancy
> Against those that afflicted him
> And made his labours of no avail.
> At the sight they shall be troubled with terrible fear
> And shall be amazed at his unexpected salvation.
> They shall say within themselves regretfully,
> Groaning in anguish of spirit :
> This it is whom we once held in derision
> And as a byword of reproach.
> We fools esteemed his life madness
> And his end without honour !
> Behold how he is reckoned among the children of God
> And his lot is among the Holy Ones.[1]
> So we erred from the way of truth
> And the light of justice did not shine upon us,
> And for us the sun did not rise.
> We satiated ourselves in the ways of lawlessness and destruction,
> And through trackless wildernesses was our path,
> But the way of the Lord we knew not ! [2]

Such views on the lot that awaits souls after their departure from this world had their inevitable repercussion on men's attitude to the miseries and sufferings of this life. As long as the religious outlook of the Israelites was this-worldly, the fortunes of men in this life could not but occupy the forefront of their thoughts. Once God's guidance had led them to the belief that after departure from this world the just would be reckoned among the Holy Ones of the heavenly court there to live for ever whereas 'the hope of the wicked is as dust

[1] The Angels are called 'the sons of God' or 'the children of God' in ob 1:6, 2:1, and 'the Holy Ones' in Job 5:1. The translation 'saints', DV and RV, is misleading

[2] Wis 5:1-7

that is carried away by the wind',[1] the whole perspective altered and man's temporal estate was seen in an entirely new light.

> For if in the sight of men they suffered chastisement,
> Their hope was full of immortality.
> After a little chastening they shall be greatly favoured,
> For God hath made trial of them,
> And found them worthy of himself.
> As gold in the furnace he tested them,
> And as a whole burnt-offering he accepted them.[2]

Thus afflictions and sufferings are no longer matter for regret and repining. They have their place in God's merciful design for man. As in the case of blessed Job, they test the sincerity of virtue, and, when borne in a spirit of filial submission, they strengthen the virtues of faith and hope and purify the life of the spirit facilitating thereby growth in the pure love of God.

[1] Wis 5:15 [2] Wis 3:4–6

Chapter X

THE TEACHING OF THE NEW TESTAMENT

The Old Testament had stressed the important, basic doctrine that all creatures are good in themselves, that all things whatsoever as created by the wisdom and power of God are apt for the purposes whereunto they are designed and are entirely harmless in themselves. This doctrine flows directly from the fact that God is Himself substantial holiness, and that all His thoughts and works springing from that substantial holiness must necessarily be themselves without any shadow of evil. Moral evil could arise in this world only through the perverted will of man applying God's good gifts to evil purposes. All things, then, being good in themselves and being created by God for the use of man and indeed handed over to the dominion of man, it was right that their value should be recognised in a spirit of gratitude to the Creator. Further, as God in His Providence had not for so many centuries revealed even to His chosen people what the state of mankind would be after death, it was inevitable that religion should be concentrated on the present life in this world and that the possession of many of God's good creatures should be regarded as a mark of His favour and wealth be held in high esteem. Thus we read in praise of Abraham that 'he had sheep and oxen and he-asses, and men-servants and maid-servants, and she-asses and camels'.[1] And similarly of Solomon it is recorded that he 'exceeded all the kings of the earth in riches' and that 'he made silver to be as plentiful in Jerusalem as stones, and cedar wood to be as common as the sycomores in the plainland'.[2] And the riches of the just and patient Job are stressed both before and after his grievous trial.

Still, though riches are good and innocent in themselves, experience taught that they can be and are abused and thus

[1] Gen 12:16 [2] 1(3) Kg 10:23, 27

become the occasion of sin. Riches expose their possessor to the danger of pride and of injustice and of oppression of the poor. The prophets were keenly aware of these evil consequences. The following lines of Isaias point to the connection between wealth and wrongdoing.

> Their land is filled with silver and gold,
> And there is no end of their treasures ;
> And their land is filled with horses,
> And their chariots are innumerable.
> Their land is full of idols ;
> They adore the work of their own hands.
> Man abases himself and bows down
> To the work of his own fingers.[1]

And the prophet Micheas denounces the injustice that springs from a desire to acquire greater wealth regardless of the rights of others.

> Out of the desire for lands they have committed robbery
> And coveting houses they have taken them for themselves.
> They oppress one and his household,
> Another and his inheritance.[2]

Such iniquity became so widespread that, as we have seen p. 78, the two terms 'the rich' and 'the wicked' became almost synonymous. Hence it was recognised that riches acquired wrongly were no blessing :

> Better the modest substance of the just man
> Than the great abundance of the wicked.[3]

And the converse equivalence of the poor and the pious shows that riches were not as a general rule looked for as the reward of piety. The many passages witnessing to God's care and protection of the poor and lowly indicate that they were not in His disfavour, but, on the contrary, were well-pleasing to Him.

[1] Is 2:7–9 [2] Mic 2:2 [3] Ps 36(37):16

The Lord shall come in judgment
With the elders of his people and its princes;
For you have consumed the vineyards,
Spoil of the poor is in your houses.
What mean you by crushing my people
And grinding the faces of the poor?[1]
Woe to them that decree decrees of wickedness,
To scribes who inscribe sentences of wrong,
To turn the weak from justice,
To rob the rights of the poor among my people![2]

And the Book of Proverbs contains a prayer which in the Old Testament context attains a remarkable degree of elevation:

Neither penury nor riches do thou appoint me;
Grant me food for my sustenance,
Lest I be sated and become faithless
And say 'Who is Yahweh?'
Or lest in penury I steal
Or utter profanely the name of my God.[3]

These lines, which embody the doctrine of the mean, prepare the way for the praise of poverty in the New Testament. Our Lord declared boldly that the state of poverty is a blessed one. His words are recorded twice: 'Blessed are the poor in spirit'[4] and 'Blessed are ye poor'.[5] As St Luke's report shows, He was addressing people who were actually poor, and this is in agreement with St Luke's following beatitude, 'Blessed are ye that hunger now'[6] though St Matthew has the form, 'Blessed are they that hunger and thirst after justice'.[7] Very likely our Lord used both forms of words on the same or different occasions. And clearly the state of poverty is not a blessing in men hankering after riches; such are not poor in spirit. But that Christ was speaking of

[1] Is 3:14 f.
[2] Is 10:1f. Cp. Mic 2:8f., Jer 22:16, Ez 16:49, Pss 73(74):19, 85(86):1f.; 131(132):15, etc.
[3] Prov 30:8f.
[4] Mt 5:3
[5] Lk 6:20
[6] Lk 6:21
[7] Mt 5:6

real poverty is shown by His advice to the rich young man 'Go sell what thou hast and give to the poor',[1] and by His denunciation of riches. 'Woe to you that are rich. . . . Woe to you that are filled'.[2] And the reason, given by our Lord in His parable of the seed, is that through the lure of wealth its possessors 'are choked with the cares and riches and pleasures of this life and yield no fruit'.[3] And for this reason 'it is hard for a rich man to enter into the kingdom of heaven'.[4]

Even without this explicit teaching the actual practice of Christ would have sufficed abundantly to make His mind perfectly plain. He had the planning and disposition of His life entirely in His own power, as St Paul reminded the Corinthians, 'You know the grace of our Lord Jesus Christ, that being rich he became poor for your sakes, that through his poverty you might be rich'.[5] Accordingly He was born in a stable, laid as an infant in a manger, and died destitute of all things. At Nazareth He was supported by the humble labour of St Joseph and of His own hands,[6] and during His public ministry He lived on alms.[7] He Himself warned a would-be follower of His poverty telling him that 'the Son of Man hath not where to lay his head'.[8]

What is the explanation of this praise and recommendation of poverty? This world and all that is in it was created by God, and all is good in itself. Why then is it laudable to renounce wealth and desire of wealth and to embrace poverty? As all is good in itself, there is clearly no obligation to give up whatever in this world is naturally desirable. But riches can easily become a snare and lead man away from God by their all-engrossing attraction. In their pursuit and enjoyment

[1] Mt 19:21 [2] Lk 6:24f. [4] Lk 8:14
[4] Mt 19:23 [5] 2 Cor 8:9
[6] Mk 6:3, 'Is not this the carpenter, the son of Mary?'
[7] Lk 8:3
[8] Mt 8:20. That this saying refers to His great poverty and not, as has been suggested, merely to His itinerant mode of life, is shown by the proposal of the scribe, who said 'Master, I will follow thee whithersoever thou goest', Mt 8:19. The man who was offering himself as a disciple evidently knew our Lord's habit of travelling from place to place and there would have been no point in an answer that merely called attention to this same fact.

religion can be lost to sight. Avarice and covetousness can be the means of setting up an idol to which man gives his service to the exclusion of his obligations to his Creator. And though wealth may not cause such shipwreck of the moral life or of Faith, it tends at least to draw the soul away from spiritual things. God's creatures tend to be a veil separating Him from our vision. The more we give ourselves to them, the more we tend to lose sight of God. And, conversely, the more we renounce creatures for God's sake, the easier it is to approach the Divine Majesty. This is why the Church in the Breviary calls riches *impedimenta*, things that tend to impede us in our journey through life from attaining our last end or from attaining it more perfectly. The embracing of poverty is then not in itself perfection but the removal of an impediment to its attainment.

Now Christ's praise of poverty and His invitation to a life of poverty, which was understood as such and followed by His disciples,[1] was an invitation to a life of hardship. Comfort is not an ally of poverty. 'Behold, they that are clothed in soft garments are in the houses of kings'.[2] Poverty is no stranger to hunger and to weariness, which are among the lesser forms of suffering. And in the scanty records we possess of the life of Christ, we find that He knew what hunger is, not only after deliberate fasting[3] but also in the course of His daily life.[4] Weariness and fatigue too were inevitable in the course of His constant journeying and preaching. He sat down on the parapet of Jacob's well exhausted after long walking,[5] and He must have been completely tired out when He slept soundly and had to be awakened by the disciples in a boat tossed by a great tempest so violent that it was covered by the waves.[6] It was from this life of hardship and its attendant suffering that the devil had attempted to withdraw him by the temptations in the wilderness. Why suffer hunger? Why not take the easy course of turning these stones into bread? Why not avoid all the trouble and exhaustion of travel and

[1] Mt 19:27. 'Behold, we have left all things and have followed thee'.
[2] Mt 11:8 [3] Mt 4:2 [4] Mt 21:19
[5] Jn 6:2 [6] Mt 8:24

continual preaching by such a manifestation of power as descending from the pinnacle of the temple into the crowded court below? But Jesus rejected such suggestions. His life was to be consonant with the end which He clearly foresaw.

What the end of His life was to be Christ hinted at first only obscurely in His talk with Nicodemus: 'As Moses lifted up the Serpent in the desert, so must the Son of Man be lifted up that whosoever believeth in him may not perish but may have life everlasting'.[1] Later, after the triumphal entry into Jerusalem, He again used the same word of Himself in speaking to the Jews: 'And I, if I be lifted up from the earth, will draw all things to myself'; and the meaning is at once made plain by St John, who adds: 'Now this he said, signifying by what death he should die',[2] In clearer language He foretold His Passion to the disciples, first, St Matthew records, after St Peter's confession: 'From that time Jesus began to show to his disciples that he must go to Jerusalem and suffer many things from the ancients and scribes and chief priests and be put to death and the third day rise again'.[3] And with more detail on the way up to the Holy City: 'Behold we go up to Jerusalem, and the Son of Man shall be betrayed to the chief priests and the scribes; and they shall condemn him to death, and shall deliver him to the Gentiles to be mocked and scourged and crucified, and the third day he shall rise again'.[4] Not only did He foretell His sufferings and death, He also proclaimed openly His complete freedom in accepting it and in accepting it for our sakes: 'I lay down my life for my sheep . . . I lay down my life that I may take it again. No man taketh it away from me, but I lay it down of myself. I have power to lay it down and I have power to take it up again'.[5] To what purpose He was to lay down His life for His sheep He expressed more clearly after the mother of the sons of Zebedee had petitioned Him for their promotion in His kingdom. Taking this manifestation of

[1] Jn 3:14f.

[2] Jn 12:32f. A variant reading of the Greek has 'I will draw all men to myself' but the sense is not essentially altered.

[3] Mt 16:21; cp. 17:12, 21f.

[4] Mt 20:18f.; cp. 20:22f.; 21:38f.

[5] Jn 10:15–18

temporal ambition as an occasion for a lesson on humility He said 'He that will be first among you shall be your servant, even as the Son of Man came not to be ministered to but to minister and to give his life a redemption for many'.[1] The meaning is that He will lay down His life a redemption for all, who in fact are many, the latter word being used, as in Isaias's prophecy of the Passion,[2] to emphasise the idea of multitude. Our Lord used the word again in the same sense at the Last Supper explaining also in part the effect of the redemption: 'This is my blood of the new testament, which shall be shed for many unto remission of sins'.[3] As Adam, our head and representative in the natural order, lost the supernatural life of grace for us all, so Christ, the second Adam,[4] our head and representative in the supernatural order, took upon Himself the sins of us all that by His Passion and death He might make satisfaction for all, reconcile us to God, and win for us again the gift of the life of grace. 'Him, who knew no sin, he hath made sin for us, that we might be made the justice of God in him'.[5] 'If, when we were enemies, we were reconciled to God by the death of his Son, much more after reconciliation shall we be saved by his life'.[6] Of the various other references in the writings of the New Testament to our redemption by the Passion of Christ may be quoted the words of the Prince of the Apostles: 'You were not redeemed with corruptible things, as gold or silver, from your vain manner of life received by tradition from your fathers, but with the precious blood of Christ, as of a lamb unspotted and undefiled'.[7] The ineffable value of this the supreme example of vicarious suffering is written large across the pages of the inspired apostolic writings. Indeed the dominant thought of Christ in those writings is that of the suffering Christ, of Christ who suffered on account of our sins for the sake of our redemption.

Now as we are all knit together into one body with Christ, into the Mystical Body of which He is the Head and we

[1] Mt 20:27f. [2] See p. 108 [3] Mt 26:28
[4] Rom 5:14 [5] 2 Cor 5:21 [6] Rom 5:10
[7] 1 Pet 1:18f.; cp. 1 Cor 6:20, 7:23, Heb 9:14, 1 Jn 1:7

the members, we must all share in the fortunes of that Body. If the Head suffers, the whole Body suffers too. 'As in one body we have many members, but all the members have not the same office, so we, being many, are one body in Christ, and every one members one of another'.[1] 'And if one member suffer anything, all the members suffer with it; or if one member is honoured, all the members rejoice with it'.[2] So the members of a Head crowned with thorns cannot expect to escape without a share of suffering. And Christ warned His disciples that so it must be. 'If the world hate you, know ye that it hath hated me before you. If you had been of the world, the world would love its own; but because you are not of the world but I have chosen you out of the world, therefore the world hateth you. Remember the word that I said to you: The servant is not greater than his master. If they have persecuted me, they will also persecute you. If they have kept watch on my speech, they will keep watch on yours also. But all these things will they do to you on account of my name'.[3] This prediction was uttered at the Last Supper. St Matthew, following his wont of grouping his materials, has recorded similar warnings at an earlier point of his narrative. 'They will deliver you up in councils and they will scourge you in their synagogues. . . . And you shall be hated by all men on account of my name. . . . And fear ye not them that kill the body and are not able to kill the soul; but rather fear him that can destroy both soul and body in hell. . . . He that taketh not up his cross and followeth me, is not worthy of me. He that findeth his life shall lose it; and he that shall lose his life for my sake shall find it'.[4]

Thus our Lord joins words of consolation to His prediction of persecutions. Those who lose their lives for His sake in this world will enter on a fuller and glorious life in the world to come. And in the Sermon on the Mount He reckons those who suffer for His sake to be fortunate and happy. 'Blessed are they that suffer persecution for justice' sake, for theirs is the kingdom of heaven. Blessed are ye when they shall revile you

[1] Rom 12:4f.
[2] 1 Cor 12:26f.
[3] Jn 15:18–21
[4] Mt 10:17, 22, 28, 38, 39

and persecute you and speak all that is evil against you, untruly, on account of my name. Be glad and rejoice, for your reward is great in heaven '.[1]

The fulfilment of Christ's prediction was not slow in coming. The history of the early church contains many examples of persecution suffered for the name of Christ. The double thread running through the Acts of the Apostles is, on the one hand, the story of the labours of the Apostles in preaching the Faith and the growth of the numbers of the Faithful, and, on the other hand, the story of the hatred and opposition that these labours and their success evoked. It may be said that wherever the Gospel was preached, persecution was aroused. Following on the stoning of St Stephen ' there was raised a great persecution against the church at Jerusalem '.[2] This was followed by persecution at Antioch in Pisidia,[3] at Iconium,[4] at Lystra,[5] at Philippi,[6] at Thessalonica,[7] at Beroea,[8] at Corinth,[9] and again at Jerusalem.[10]

These persecutions did not stop the progress of the Faith or break the spirit of the Christians. They had taken our Lord's words to heart that it is a noble thing to suffer for His sake. When the Apostles had been scourged by order of the Sanhedrin and forbidden to speak in the name of Jesus ' they went from the presence of the council rejoicing that they were accounted worthy to suffer reproach for the name of Jesus ; and they ceased not every day, in the temple and from house to house, to teach and preach Christ Jesus '.[11] This is an example of pure, unselfish love. The Apostles rejoiced, not because suffering borne for Christ would bring its great reward, but because in their personal devotion to Christ they were glad to endure some measure of the suffering He had endured, and to endure it in His cause. He had suffered for them ; they counted it joy to suffer for Him. Love issuing thus in joy at pain suffered for the One beloved is understood not by the intellect but by the heart. Only he who knows

[1] Mt 5:10–12
[2] Acts 7:59, 8:1–3
[3] 13:50
[4] 14:4–6
[5] 14:18 (RV 19)
[6] 6, 16:19–24
[7] 17:5–9
[8] 17:13
[9] 18:12–17
[10] 21:27ff., 22:22, 23:12ff., 25:3
[11] Acts 5:41f.

such love will understand. This love was strong also in St Paul. 'We suffer persecution, but we are not forsaken. We are cast down, but we perish not. Always bearing about in our body the dying of Jesus that the life also of Jesus may be made manifest in our bodies. For we who live are always being delivered unto death for Jesus' sake that the life also of Jesus may be made manifest in our mortal flesh'.[1] And again: 'Gladly therefore will I glory in my infirmities that the power of Christ may dwell in me. Wherefore I find pleasure in infirmities, in reproaches, in necessities, in persecutions, in distresses, for Christ; for when I am weak, then am I strong'.[2]

This conformity with Christ's sufferings moved also the hearts of the Faithful, as may be judged from the fact that their pastors did not consider this motive too elevated to put before them. 'Unto you', wrote St Paul to the Philippians, 'it is given for Christ, not only to believe in him, but also to suffer for him'.[3] So also St Peter: 'This is a grace, if a man endure sorrows suffering wrongfully on account of his sense of duty to God. . . . If you do right and suffer patiently, this is acceptable with God. For unto this have you been called, because Christ also suffered for you leaving you an example that you should follow in his footsteps, who committed no sin, neither was guile found in his mouth'.[4]

In addition to this sublime motive of the imitation of Christ and conformity with Him in His sufferings the Apostles put also other considerations before the Christians committed to their charge. As the members of the Mystical Body whose Head was the subject of such great sufferings, could not but suffer in union with Him,[5] and the sufferings of one member are the sufferings of the whole body, so the sufferings of Christ's members, of the members of His Mystical Body, which is the Church, are also Christ's sufferings. And this our Lord Himself signified to St Paul by His question 'Saul, Saul, why persecutest thou me?'[6] He did not ask, 'Why persecutest thou my followers?' or 'Why persecutest thou my Church?' but 'Why persecutest thou me?', thus showing His unity

[1] 2 Cor 4:9–11
[2] 2 Cor 12:9f.
[3] Phil 1:29
[4] 1 Pet 2:19–22
[5] See p. 134
[6] Acts 9:4

with the Church, identifying Himself with the Church. And so St Paul could speak of the personal sufferings of Christ not being complete, of something being lacking to them. 'I rejoice now in my sufferings for you and am filling up those things that are wanting of the afflictions of Christ, in my flesh for his body which is the Church '.[1] It may be noted that the translations 'I fill up' (DV and RV) and 'I make up' (WV) rather suggest that Paul's own sufferings sufficed to supply all that was wanting, but such was not his thought nor indeed that of the translators. Paul was sharing in a process which is common to all true Christians, and the members of the Church today are still doing their part in filling up what was lacking to the sufferings of Christ. Not that anything was lacking to the atoning power of the Passion of Christ. The sufferings and death of God made Man were of infinite value and superabundantly sufficed for the redemption of the world. 'Christ died for us. . . . We were reconciled to God by the death of his Son '.[2] But Christ deigned to leave some share of His work and of His sufferings to His members, not to redeem the world, but to act as His ministers in the application to men of the atoning power of His redemption. So this too is a consolation for Christians of all ages that their sufferings borne as Christians are Christ's sufferings and are accepted by Him as sharing in His sufferings to make His redemption effectual for the salvation of men.

Further the Apostles did not neglect to console the Faithful in their tribulations by the consideration that they provide a testing of virtue which, in those who stand the test, leads to an increase and strengthening of virtue, just as the testing of Abraham's faith and love through the order to sacrifice his son made his faith and love the stronger and the more enduring. 'We glory in tribulations, knowing that tribulation worketh endurance, and endurance tried virtue, and tried virtue hope; and hope does not put to shame, because the charity of God is poured forth in our hearts by the Holy Ghost who is given to us '.[3] Tribulation gives an opportunity to exercise constancy and perseverance in the practice of patience, which is

[1] Col 1:24 [2] Rom 5:9–10 [3] Rom 5:3–5

the Christian virtue of enduring suffering at least with resignation. And if the tribulation is borne with this Christian endurance, the test issues in tried, strengthened and genuine virtue, which gives every ground for hope ; and hope does not put to shame, because it will not disappoint. And our hope cannot mock us because the love God has for us is poured into our hearts. In a word, trials and tribulations are God-given opportunities to practise and thereby to strengthen virtue.

St James writes in the same sense : ' My brethren, count it all joy, when you fall into divers trials, knowing that the testing of your faith worketh patience, and let patience have its perfect effect that you may be perfect and entire, lacking in nothing '.[1] The doctine, it will be seen, is the same as that of St Paul to the Romans just quoted.

Here may be quoted a text from the Epistle to the Hebrews : Christ ' though he was Son, learnt obedience by his sufferings '.[2] As a divine person He was infinitely perfect with all the perfection of God Incarnate, and the meaning therefore is not that He learnt the virtue of obedience or its moral value. But as a Man He learnt in His human experience what obedience may entail, Himself ' becoming obedient unto death, even to the death of the cross '.[3] He knew by His own experience and suffering the full difficulty and hardship of whatever He might ask of His followers. He asks of us nothing that He did not first endure Himself. ' We have not a high-priest who cannot have compassion on our infirmities, but one tried in all things as we are, without sin '.[4] To quote Cornelius a Lapide : ' Christ learnt obedience by suffering to show that obedience, patience, and other virtues are learnt by men far better, more fully and more efficaciously by suffering and their exercise than by reasoning ; truly *τὰ παθήματα μαθήματα*, sufferings are the best lessons and instructions. And, as St Bernard says, Epist. 88, " Humiliation is the road that leads to humility, as patience to peace, as reading to knowledge. If you see the virtue of humility, do not refuse the road of humiliation. For if you do not suffer yourself to be humiliated, you cannot advance to humility ". In our passage the Apostle stresses obedience to the

[1] Jas 1:2–4 [2] Heb 5:8 [3] Phil 2:8 [4] Heb 4:15

Hebrews above other virtues in order that they may imitate it and learn to obey God and Christ with constancy even if thereby they have to undergo and suffer spoliation, exile, and even death itself'.[1]

The Epistle to the Hebrews contains another, lengthy exhortation to endurance and patience in tribulations and sufferings : 'Let us with patience run the race lying before us, looking on Jesus, the author and finisher of faith, who, for the joy set before him, endured the cross, despising the shame, and now sitteth on the right hand of the throne of God. For think diligently upon him that endured such opposition from sinners against himself, that you be not wearied fainting in your minds. For you have not yet resisted unto blood striving against sin. And you have forgotten the consolation that speaketh unto you as unto sons, saying :

My son, do not esteem lightly the chastening of the Lord,
Neither be thou fainthearted when rebuked by him ;
For whom the Lord loveth, he chasteneth,
And scourgeth every son whom he receiveth.[2]

What you endure is for correction. God dealeth with you as with sons ; for what son is there whom his father does not correct ? But if you be without correction, of which all have a share, then are you bastards and not sons. Moreover, we had the fathers of our flesh for correctors and we reverenced them. Shall we not much rather be subject to the Father of spirits and live ? For they corrected us for a few days according as it seemed good to them, but he for our profit that we may partake of his holiness. Now all correction seemeth for the moment to be matter not of joy but of pain but afterwards it giveth in return to those exercised by it the peaceful fruit of righteousness'.[3]

Our Lord is here said to have endured the cross 'for the joy set before him', words which appear to allude to the wonderful incident of the Angel's apparition to Him during the agony in the garden. He was praying 'Father, if thou

[1] From Cornelius a Lapide's commentary on this passage
[2] Prov 3:11–12 according to the Septuagint [3] Heb 12:1–11

wilt, remove this chalice from me; but yet not my will but thine be done'. Then while He yet prayed, 'there appear to him an angel from heaven strengthening him; and being in an agony he prayed the longer'.[1] This is recorded by St Luke, the friend and companion of St Paul, and it seems that here in the Epistle to the Hebrews we are given an indication of some part of the consoling message brought by the Angel. That Christ deigned to be comforted by an Angel, indeed that He could be comforted by one of His creatures, shows how completely true it is that He became man like unto us, sin only excepted. The expression used 'for the joy set before him' ἀντὶ τῆς χαρᾶς is of the same form as that which occurs later in the chapter ἀντὶ βρώσεως μιᾶς 'Esau who for one mess sold his first birthright'.[2] In each case the preposition denotes the acceptance of one thing in lieu of another. Cornelius a Lapide thinks that the joy set before Christ was His glorious Resurrection and the salvation of men. The latter thought has its foundation in the triumphal conclusion of the Passion-Psalm which our Lord recited on the Cross:

> All the ends of the earth shall remember
> And shall be converted to the Lord;
> For the kingdom is the Lord's,
> And he shall have dominion over the nations.[3]

So too in the sequel of Isaias's prophecy of the Passion:

> He shall see a long-lived seed;
> And the will of the Lord shall be prosperous in his hand.[4]

In both these celebrated predictions the subsequent triumph of the suffering Messias is described in immediate connection with His foregoing mockery, anguish, and pains. And it may well be that the Angel set these passages of the inspired word before Christ as He lay in His sweat of blood in the garden of Gethsemani.

Still more do we, weak vessels, stand in need of consolation. This the Apostles knew and they did not hesitate to

[1] Lk 22:42f. [2] Heb 12:16 [3] Ps 21(22):28f. [4] Is 53:10

encourage their disciples with the thought of the reward of happiness and glory that awaited them. 'The Spirit himself giveth testimony to our spirit that we are the sons of God. And if sons, heirs also; heirs indeed of God, and joint heirs with Christ, yet so, if we suffer with him that we may also be glorified with him. For I reckon that the sufferings of this time are not worthy to be compared with the glory to come that shall be revealed in us'.[1] So again St Paul writes to the Corinthians: 'Our present light tribulation worketh for us above measure exceedingly an eternal weight of glory'.[2] 'If we endure, we shall also reign with him'.[3] And the glory which came to Christ through His Passion and Death is held up as an example, for the members must share, as in the sufferings, so also in the glory of their Head. 'We see Jesus, who was made a little lower than the angels, for the suffering of death crowned with glory and honour, that through the grace of God he might taste death for all; for it became him for whom are all things and by whom are all things, who brought many sons unto glory, to bring to consummation the author of their salvation by his passion'.[4] Jesus was brought to consummation or to the perfection due to Him by being crowned with honour and glory.

The texts considered hitherto in this chapter have been concerned with the sufferings that come to men and women unsought, either through the instrumentality of other human beings as in religious persecutions or through natural causes beyond the control of man. But the New Testament doctrine extends beyond these to sufferings voluntarily undertaken. These may be negative as in the refusal to gratify legitimate physical desires and cravings, or they may be positive as in discomfort or pain deliberately self-inflicted. There are illegitimate bodily cravings, the gratification of which would be against the laws of God and sinful. For, as St Paul expresses it, 'I delight in the law of God according to the inward man, but I perceive another law in my members fighting against the law of my mind'.[5] That is to say, man's irrational, lower,

[1] Rom 8:16–18
[2] 2 Cor 4:17
[3] 2 Tim 2:12
[4] Heb 2:9f.
[5] Rom 7:22f.

animal nature has impulses which are contrary to the dictates of conscience and the gratification of which would be sinful. Hence it is that 'the flesh lusteth against the spirit and the spirit against the flesh, for these are contrary one to another'.[1] Now souls who are in earnest in this struggle against the flesh and its cravings are anxious to increase their powers of resistance. This they do by the voluntary refusal to yield to bodily desires in matters which are entirely legitimate. In this way they acquire greater control over their lower nature. Clearly a person who is accustomed to refuse himself gratifications which are lawful will be all the stronger and more alert to refuse himself gratifications which would be unlawful and sinful. The spirit and practice of such self-control in matters where there is no question of sin is called asceticism. This word according to its derivation from the Greek denotes the practising, training, exercising of self-control to acquire new strength in the struggle against whatever might be an impediment in the service of God.

St Timothy was practising self-abnegation of this type by restricting himself to the use of water, but, as all such mortifications must be controlled by prudence, St Paul judged that his state of health required some relaxation of this austerity: 'Do not continue drinking water, but use a little wine for thy stomach's sake and thy frequent infirmities'.[2] But he was in no way opposed to such asceticism in itself. On the contrary, he reminded his converts of the strict abstinence practised by athletes that their example might stimulate them to similar self-control for the higher end of victory in the spiritual contest. 'Every man that striveth in the games refraineth himself in all things; and they indeed that they may receive a corruptible crown, but we an incorruptible one. . . . I chastise my body, lest having preached to others I myself should become a castaway'.[3] The word here translated 'chastise' (DV; Vulgate 'castigo'; RV 'buffet') properly means 'to strike below the eyes, give a black eye', but came to be used with the weakened sense of 'illtreat, vex'. It is so used in the parable of the unjust judge: 'because this widow is trouble-

[1] Gal 5:17 [2] 1 Tim 5:23 [3] 1 Cor 9:25–27

some to me, I will avenge her, lest continually coming she weary me' (DV; RV 'wear me out').[1] It does not, therefore, here necessarily denote more than that St Paul used his body hardly, denying it luxuries and comforts and forcing it to undergo grave discomforts 'in labour and hardships, in watchings often, in hunger and thirst, in fastings often, in cold and nakedness'.[2]

In this last-cited passage St Paul distinguishes between his endurance of hunger and thirst and his fasting, the former referring to occasions when circumstances allowed him nothing to eat or drink and the latter to his voluntary abstinence from food. Such fasting was a well-established custom among the Jews. It will be remembered that the disciples of John asked our Lord 'Why do we and the Pharisees fast often but thy disciples do not fast?'[3] But our Lord accused the hypocrites of fasting out of human respect merely to be admired and, as He repeatedly called the scribes and Pharisees hypocrites,[4] there can be no doubt of whom He spoke: 'When you fast, be not as the hypocrites sad-faced, for they disfigure their faces that they may be seen by men to be fasting. Amen I say to you, they have received their reward. But thou, when thou fastest, anoint thy head and wash thy face, that thou be not seen by men to be fasting but by thy Father who is in secret, and thy Father who seeth in secret will repay thee'.[5] But not all Jews were hypocrites, certainly not holy Anna the prophetess 'who departed not from the temple by fastings and prayers serving night and day'.[6] So too 'John the Baptist came neither eating bread nor drinking wine',[7] And our Lord gave an example to His disciples when He 'fasted forty days and forty nights',[8] or, as St Luke puts it in negative form, 'he ate nothing in those days'.[9] And He indicated His approval of fasting by His disciples, indeed His will that they should fast in His reply to the question, quoted just above, which was put to Him by the disciples of John: 'Can the children of the bridegroom mourn as long as the

[1] Lk 18:5
[2] 2 Cor 11:27
[3] Mt 9:14
[4] Mt chap. 23
[5] Mt 6:16–18
[6] Lk 2:37
[7] Lk 7:33
[8] Mt 4:2
[9] Lk 4:2

bridegroom is with them? But the days will come when the bridegroom shall be taken away from them; and then they shall fast'.[1] The answer was peculiarly apt in reply to the followers of the Baptist for he had called Jesus the bridegroom and himself 'the friend of the bridegroom, who standeth and heareth him (and) rejoiceth with joy because of the bridegroom's voice'.[2] It was the custom of the Jews not to fast during the bridal feast even if the great fast of the day of Atonement fell during the period. Accordingly after the Ascension the practice of fasting was in use among the early Christians.[3] And St Paul exhorts the Corinthians thereto: 'In everything let us commend ourselves as the ministers of God in much patience, in tribulations, in necessities, in distresses, in stripes, in prisons, in seditions, in labours, in watchings, in fastings'.[4]

Among other ascetic practices commended in the New Testament is the deliberate choice of the state of virginity. This is insistently eulogised by St Paul.[5] He also commends temporary abstinence to married people.[6] This commendation of virginity is based on our Lord's own teaching: 'There are eunuchs who have made themselves eunuchs for the sake of the kingdom of heaven'.[7] The term is here used metaphorically of voluntary celibacy, for which a special grace of God is required: 'Not all are equal to this saying, but they to whom it is given. . . . He that can take, let him take it'.[8] That the grace was given and accepted by many may be inferred from the passage in the Apocalypse where St John speaks of the virgins who 'follow the Lamb whithersoever he goeth. These were purchased from among men, firstfruits to God and to the Lamb'.[9]

Very remarkable is the spirit of detachment from temporal advantages which reigned in the early Church. So strong was this that the Faithful at Jerusalem willingly sold their land and houses for the support of their needy brethren.[10] This was in accord with the love of poverty preached by Christ:

[1] Mt 9:15 [2] Jn 3:29 [3] Acts 13:2f.; 14:22
[4] 2 Cor 6:4f. [5] 1 Cor 7:1, 7–8, 25–8, 32–5, 38 [6] 1 Cor 7:5
[7] Mt 19:12 [8] Mt 19:11f. [9] Apoc 14:4 [10] Acts 4:32–7

'Every one that hath left houses . . . or lands for my name's sake shall receive a hundredfold and shall inherit life everlasting'.[1] The sad story of Ananias and Sapphira, who sold their land but secretly kept back part of the price for their own use,[2] seems to warrant the inference that they acted as they did to avoid singularity. If this was in fact their motive, it shows that the renunciation of property was well-nigh universal: 'Neither did any one say that aught of his possessions was his own, but they had all things in common'.[3]

The spirit that prompted this generous renunciation and community of property is entirely in agreement with the teaching of our Lord, but experience showed that the actual method adopted could not be imitated. By selling their houses and lands and thus using their capital for current needs the community at Jerusalem was quickly reduced to such straits that they became dependent for their support on alms sent from other Churches.[4]

In addition to specific invitations to Christian asceticism our Lord proposed the all-embracing exhortation, 'If any man will come after me, let him deny himself and take up his cross and follow me'.[5] This phrase 'deny himself' is sometimes misunderstood as if it meant 'to deny (whatever it may be) to himself'.[6] This sense of denying oneself pleasure and gratification is certainly included in the phrase or rather is to be legitimately deduced from it. But it is not the primary meaning for the reason that the pronoun is not in the dative but in the accusative. It is the direct object of the verb. And the meaning of the phrase may be deduced from the Passion narrative where the same verb is again used with the pronoun

[1] Mt 19:29 [2] Acts 5:1–11 [3] Acts 4:32

[4] 1 Cor 16:1–4, 2 Cor 9:1–15, Acts 24:17. On the Jewish sect at Alexandria whose way of life is described by Philo, *De Vita Contemplativa*, and whom Eusebius, *Hist. Eccl.* II 16, and St Jerome, *De Viris Illustr.* 8 and 11 (Migne, PL 23:621f., 625f.) thought to be a Christian community founded by St Mark, see the article 'Therapeutai' in Pauly-Wissowa, vol. V A.

[5] Mt 16:24, Mk 8:34, Lk 9:23; cp. Mt 10:38 'He that taketh not up his cross and followeth me is not worthy of me', and Lk 14:27 'Whosoever doth not carry his cross and come after me cannot be my disciple'.

[6] An example of this misconstruction may be seen in the Oxford English Dictionary under the word 'deny'.

in the accusative. Our Lord foretold Peter's denials: 'Amen I say to thee that in this night before the cock crow thou wilt deny me thrice'.[1] Now Peter's denial of our Lord was a disavowal of Him, a repudiation, a denial that he knew Him. So too in our Lord's words 'He that shall deny me before men shall be denied before the angels of God'.[2] That is to say, he who disavows Christ before men will be disavowed in the judgment. Christ will say 'I know you not'.[3] So we are invited to treat ourselves as if we did not know ourselves and were not interested in ourselves. And that is how St John Chrysostom explains this saying of Christ, which was addressed not to a select body of disciples (Mt) only but also to the multitude (Mk), even to all (Lk). 'Let us see what it is to deny oneself. But first let us learn what it is to deny another and then we shall know what it is to deny oneself. What then is it to deny another? He who denies another, whether a brother or a domestic or whoever it may be, if he sees him being flogged or being thrown into chains or led away to execution or suffering whatever it may be, does not defend him, does not help him, is not moved to pity, feels no sympathy with him, being once and for all alienated from him. In this way, then, He wishes us to reck nothing of our own body, whether they flog it or strike it or burn it or do anything whatsoever. . . . Christ did not say "Let him not spare himself" but with a more emphatic word "Let him deny himself", that is, let him have no interest in himself but give himself up to dangers, to struggles, and let him be so disposed as if someone else was the victim'.[4] This, it should be noted, is part of an address to a mixed congregation.

And now an extract from the homily of St Gregory the Great which he preached to the people in the basilica of SS Processus and Martinianus on the feast of those Saints. 'It is not enough to leave our possessions unless we also leave ourselves. What is the meaning of leaving ourselves? For if we leave ourselves, where shall we go outside of ourselves?

[1] Mt 26:34-5, 75, Mk 14:30-1, 72, Lk 22:34, 61
[2] Lk 12:9 [3] Mt 25:12
[4] *Hom.* 56 (*al.* 55) *in Matthaeum* (Migne, PG 58:541f.)

Or who is it who goes, if a man has left himself? But we are one thing through our fall into sin, a different thing as we were made by nature; what we have made is one thing, what we were made is another. Let us leave ourselves such as we have made ourselves by sin, and let us remain ourselves such as we were made by grace. For, see, if he who was proud is converted to Christ and becomes humble, he leaves himself. If a lustful man has changed his life to continence, he has surely denied what he was. If an avaricious man has ceased to be covetous, and he has learnt to distribute his own goods who formerly robbed those of others, without doubt he has left himself. He is indeed himself by nature but he is not himself by malice. . . . So then we leave ourselves, then we deny ourselves, when we avoid what we were by our old way of life and strive to attain the newness of life to which we are called'.[1]

These two expositions of this saying of our Saviour proceed on very different lines. Each gives part of the meaning and they mutually supplement each other.

To complete this survey of the New Testament doctrine on suffering it remains to add that here also, as in the Old Testament, it is sometimes the punishment of sin. Thus the priest Zachary, though his blameless life is praised, was struck with dumbness because of his refusal to believe the words of the Angel.[2] Herod Agrippa, who had put James, the brother of John to death and purposed to execute St Peter also, was visited with a more terrible punishment. As he was sitting on the judgement seat 'the people made acclamation, saying: It is the voice of a god and not of a man. And forthwith an angel of the Lord struck him, because he had not given the honour to God, and becoming eaten up by worms he gave up the ghost'.[3] A third example is provided by the story of Elymas, who tried to prevent the proconsul Sergius Paulus from embracing the Faith. St Paul accused him of not ceasing 'to pervert the right ways of the Lord', and added: 'And now behold, the hand of the Lord is upon thee, and thou shalt be blind, not seeing for a time'. Then the narrative continues:

[1] *Homiliae in Evangelia* 32 n. 2 (Migne PL 76:123)
[2] Lk 1:6, 20 [3] Acts 12:22f.

'Immediately there fell a mist and darkness upon him, and going about he sought someone to lead him by the hand'.[1]

The old idea that all suffering and calamities are the fruit of sin still persisted, but this doctrine our Lord repudiated on more than one occasion. When some told him of the Galileans, whose blood Pilate had mingled with their sacrifices, he answered, 'Think you that these Galileans were sinners above all the men of Galilee because they suffered thus? No, I say to you, but unless you repent, you shall all likewise perish. Or those eighteen on whom the tower fell in Siloe and slew them, think you that they were debtors above all the inhabitants of Jerusalem? No, I say to you, but unless you repent, you shall all likewise perish'.[2] The word 'debtors' is here used in the sense of 'sinners', debtors to God. It is the same word ὀφειλέται that is used in St Matthew's version of the 'Our Father': 'Forgive us our debts as we also forgive our debtors'.[3]

The other occasion on which our Saviour repudiated the false doctrine is recorded by St John. 'Jesus passing by saw a man who was blind from his birth, and his disciples asked him: Rabbi, who sinned, this man or his parents, that he should be born blind? Jesus answered: Neither did this man sin nor his parents, but that the works of God should be made manifest in him'.[4] Our Lord's answer does not mean that neither the man nor his parents had been guilty of any sin but that they had committed no sin that was punished by the congenital blindness. The wonderful works of God were made manifest in the blind man when Christ, who was 'the light of the world', gave him back the use of his eyes, which He had called 'the light of the body'.[5] Such manifestations of God's works were for the good of mankind in general and of this blind man in particular. The benefit was exclusively for man. And we may well believe that it was better for the blind man himself to have been so born considering the spiritual enlightenment and grace of which his cure was the occasion. And

[1] Acts 13:10f. [2] Lk 13:1–5 [3] Mt 6:12
[4] Jn 9:1–3. On the disciples' question, see further Appendix I
[5] Jn 9:5 and Mt 6:22

although the affliction was directed by divine Providence to a higher religious purpose, there is no reason to suppose that in itself it was due to any but purely natural causes which, given the required conjunction of circumstances, would have produced the same disability in any other man. With the words of Christ here, that 'the works of God should be made manifest' in the blind man, may be compared what He said of the sickness of Lazarus: 'This sickness is not unto death but for the glory of God that the Son of God may be glorified by it'.[1] In this case the work and glory of God was manifested by the resuscitation of Lazarus from the dead. And this manifestation had two effects which are noted in the Gospel. It gave occasion of faith in Jesus among the Jews: 'Many of the Jews who had come to Mary and had seen what Jesus did, believed in him'.[2] And on the other hand it was the occasion of the decision of the Jews to put our Lord to death. 'The chief priests, therefore, and the Pharisees gathered a council and said: What do we, for this man doth many miracles? . . . From that day therefore they devised to put him to death'.[3] In these ways God was glorified in the Son of God that many conceived faith in Him and He laid down His life for the redemption of us all. Once more the gain was all for the benefit of man. As St Augustine put it 'Talis glorificatio non ipsum auxit sed nobis profuit', that is, through such glorification nothing accrued to God but benefit to us.

The falsity of the belief in the necessary connection between misfortune and sin is further shown by St Luke's narrative in the Acts. After the shipwreck on the coast of Malta 'when Paul had gathered together a bundle of sticks and had laid them on the fire, a viper came out of the heat and fastened on his hand. And when the barbarians saw the beast hanging from his hand, they said to one another: Undoubtedly this man is a murderer. Though he hath escaped from the sea, vengeance doth not suffer him to live. But the shook the beast off into the fire and suffered no harm'.[4] The natives are here called 'barbarians' not that they were a quite uncivilised people, but, in accordance with the Greek phraseology,

[1] Jn 11:4 [2] Jn 11:45 [3] Jn 11:47, 53 [4] Acts 28:3–5

because their language was Phoenician, a non-Greek idiom. The Phoenicians were a Semitic people and neighbours of the Hebrews, with whom they shared in many ways a common culture and outlook on life.

The New Testament doctrine on the subject of suffering comes to a fitting close with St John's vision of the glory and happy lot that await those who have endured to the end in the cause of righteousness. 'These that are clothed in white robes, who are they? And whence came they? . . . These are they who are come out of the great tribulation and have washed their robes and have made them white in the blood of the Lamb. Therefore they are before the throne of God, and they serve him day and night in his temple. And he that sitteth on the throne shall spread his tabernacle over them. And they shall no more hunger nor shall they thirst more; neither shall the sun fall on them nor any heat, for the Lamb, which is in the midst of the throne, shall be their shepherd and shall lead them to the fountains of the waters of life; and God shall wipe away all tears from their eyes'.[1] 'Blessed are the dead who die in the Lord from henceforth. Yea, saith the Spirit, that they may rest from their labours; for their works follow with them'.[2]

APPENDIX I: NOTE ON JOHN 9:2.

In what sense did the disciples imagine that the man could have been born blind on account of any sin of his own? This is an old problem of which several solutions have been offered. Josephus has been understood to say that the Pharisees believed in metempsychosis; but this is a misconstruction of his meaning. What he says is this: According to the teaching of the Pharisees 'all souls are incorruptible [that is, immortal], but only the souls of the good pass into another body whereas those of the evil are punished with everlasting retribution', *Bellum Judaicum* II viii 14. And this fully agrees with what he writes elsewhere: 'Their belief is that souls are possessed of an immortal power and that under the earth there are punish-

[1] Apoc 7:13–17 [2] Apoc 14:13

ments and honours for those who during life practised virtue or wickedness, and for the latter there is moreover eternal imprisonment, but for the former the release of a new life', *Antiquitates Judaicae* XVIII i 3. The difference between the two passages is that the latter speaks of the intervening interval of time before the coming of the expected Messias, and the former of the Messianic age. Thus the statement that the souls of the good pass into another body has nothing in common with the doctrine of the transmigration of souls, but means that they will rise again with new bodies in the time of the Messias. In any case, even if Josephus had spoken of the transmigration of souls, this passage would not explain the question of the disciples, as according to the Jewish historian only the souls of the good pass into another body, whereas the question of the disciples supposes the sinfulness of the man born blind.

St Cyril of Alexandria mentions, only to reject, another opinion according to which the sin was committed during a pre-existence of the soul before it was united to the body, *In Joannis Evang.* (PG 73:911). This was the view of Origen who held that Adam and Eve were created as pure spirits and were afterwards incarcerated in bodies as a punishment of their sin and were at the same time brought down to dwell on earth. Among the Jewish Rabbis this opinion of the pre-existence of souls first appears in the third Christian century, and is then so meagrely attested that it provides no evidence of a belief prevalent two centuries earlier, H. L. Strack-P.Billerbeck, *Kommentar zum Neuen Testament aus Talmud und Midrasch* II (München 1924) 528.[1]

A third opinion would explain the question by reference to some sin committed by the infant in its mother's womb before birth. So J. Lightfoot, *Opera Omnia* II (Roterodami 1686) 639. But the only passages which attest the belief among the Jews in the possibility of such a sin deal with the struggling of Esau and Jacob in the womb of Rebecca, Gen 25:22, Strack-Billerbeck, 528. This is altogether too special a case to warrant a belief among the Jews of more than the abstract possibility of such a sin.

[1] See also Appendix II

A fourth suggestion was made by Theodore of Mopsuestia, *In Evang. Joan.* (Migne, PG 66:753A). According to this, the blindness was due to God's foreknowledge of some wickedness of which the man would be guilty some time after birth. This view has found no favour.

There remains as most plausible the opinion of J. Knabenbauer, S.J., *Evang. sec. Joan.* (Parisiis 1898) 307. The disciples had no definite idea in their minds how the man himself could have merited the blindness but proposed their question who had sinned without previously thrashing the matter out in their minds.

Appendix II: A Note on Wisdom 8:19–20

Further evidence that the disciples might in fact have thought of some sin committed by the blind man in a previous existence might be brought from Philo, whose works in various passages reflect his belief in the pre-existence of souls, and from the alleged doctrine of the Book of Wisdom.

Of Philo's theory there is no doubt, but his views were so personal and so divergent from the standard beliefs of Judaism that they are no indication of the prevalence of such views and cannot be legitimately used as guides to the meaning of other writers. He lived at Alexandria in the first Christian century and was a contemporary of our Lord's. He attempted a fusion of Greek philosophy with the tenets of Judaism and sought support for them in the Hebrew Scriptures by a bold use of allegory. His doctrine of pre-existence was based on that of Plato.

According to the teaching of the Greek philosopher there are established harmonies in the universe, each thing being harmoniously disposed within itself and also externally in its relation to other things. Among such planned harmonies, however, there was no internal disposition in souls to be united with bodies. On the contrary, souls, equal in number to the stars, ranged freely through the whole heaven without any pre-determined tendency to conjunction with bodies. And only those dragged down by vice or forgetfulness of true realities descend to this earth. Once arrived here below they are obliged by a fixed law to take up their abode in a human frame. No true union of the two elements results, not even the friendly relation of host and guest. But the soul finds itself enshrined in a living tomb, imprisoned in the body. At the end of this first life there follows a judgment. Some souls go down to a subterranean abode for correction and punishment; others return to some place in heaven. After a period of a thousand years the souls are given a free choice. They may pass again into a human form or into that of a beast. Only the soul that has never seen the truth will not pass into the human form, and this not precisely as a punishment but because man should have universal concepts. But eventually a soul from a brute animal may pass into a man. Such, at least, are the ideas sketched on this subject of transmigration in the *Phraedrus*, whereas in the *Timaeus* the penalty of a bad life is to pass first into the body of a woman, and after renewed evil-doing even into that of a beast.[1]

The doctrine of Philo is closely modelled on this teaching of Plato's. The air is full of bodiless souls, it being the design of the Creator that every part of the universe should have its inhabitants and the air being the dwelling-place most suited to souls. They are incorruptible and immortal. and equal in number to the stars. Some of them having an attraction to bodies and earthly things descend to be bound up in mortal bodies. Some return to the upper regions. Of these some come back to earth filled with longing for the mortal life they have become familiar with, whereas others are persuaded of the futility of such an existence and pronounce the body a prison and a tomb. They escape as it were from confinement and rise aloft to range through the ether. In addition to these souls that have tasted human life, whether with pleasure or disgust, others, the best and purest, never felt any attraction to this earth and never came down from their abode above.

[1] *Phaedrus* 245–50; *Timaeus* 40–2. Some other points show a wavering of thought on Plato's part. According to the *Timaeus* the souls were formed by the Creator who made also the lesser gods, both visible and invisible. According to the *Phaedrus*, on the other hand, souls are both immortal and without beginning.

These are the Angels. The body is an abominable prison and its jailers are pleasures, desires and cravings. It is a leathern burden, which God knows to be evil, a plotter against the soul, a corpse without life. What we human beings do is to carry a corpse about, the soul having strength enough without trouble to carry the body, which of itself is a dead thing.[1]

Important points of this teaching are in direct opposition to the Hebrew Scriptures though professedly based thereon by way of allegory. So far from souls having been created before bodies, according to the account in Gen 2:7 God formed first the lifeless body of Adam and breathed into its nostrils the breath of life, and thus Adam became a living being. Neither is there any hint that souls were created for an independent existence with no natural disposition to form with bodies living human beings. Neither do the ancient Scriptures give any warrant for the idea that the souls of men are of just the same nature as the Angels and differ from them only in degree of virtue. The idea that the soul is imprisoned in the body is also quite alien to ancient Hebrew thought. On the contrary, man, as he came forth from the hands of God, was good like all the other works created by God. And it was God Himself who placed the spirit of life in the human body and so caused it to live. And it was not the body that occasioned the first sin. It was a sin of pride, conceived in the mind, the foolish desire to be like to God.

Philo, it is clear, was a thinker who stood outside the regular Jewish tradition. He set out his ideas clearly and attempted to find a basis for them in Holy Scripture. He is not, therefore, a writer whose doctrines it would be right to suppose to be those of another Jewish author, even if contemporary or later, without adequate indications. Such a supposition has, however, been entertained of the author of the Book of Wisdom. Neither the date nor the place of origin of the book are known with certainty. It is admitted with almost complete unanimity that it antedates the writings of Philo, and most date it about 50 B.C. or earlier. It is commonly

[1] *De Somniis* I 135–41 ; *De Migratione Abrahae* 9 ; *De Gigantibus* 6–16 ; *De Legum Allegoriis* III 69

thought that the writer lived in Alexandria. Even if this were established with certainty, it would not of itself suffice to prove even the probability that the doctrine of the pre-existence of souls was known to and still less that it was accepted by the author. The passage in question is the following :

> παῖς δὲ ἤμην εὐφυής,
> ψυχῆς τε ἔλαχον ἀγαθῆς,
> μᾶλλον δὲ ἀγαθὸς ὢν ἦλθον εἰς σῶμα ἀμίαντον.

The RV translates :

> Now I was a child of parts, and a good soul fell to my lot ;
> Nay rather, being good, I came into a body undefiled.

For 'a child of parts' the margin suggests the alternative 'a goodly child'. The word εὐφυής properly means 'well-grown' and is used, for instance, by Aristotle of hands and feet in a context which demands the meaning 'suitably grown' for a given purpose.[1] It also came to be used of a good natural disposition. Thus Aristotle applies it to Laconian bitches as gentler and more docile than dogs.[2] As the whole context is in praise of wisdom and the importance of acquiring it, it might seem that this meaning is that here intended as more important for the purpose than bodily perfection. This is not so certain, however, as a healthy mind in a healthy body is the instrument best fitted for the acquisition of wisdom. And, moreover, if the word is understood of mental and moral characteristics, the following clause becomes practically tautological. As, for the Hebrews, the person was the whole human being, the 'living being' of Gen 2:7, it may be considered certain that both elements of man are included in this verse 19. The two clauses of the sentence united by the enclitic τε, which closely unites the elements it affects, constitutes a complete enunciation of what the writer had in mind to say, namely, that though he had all the natural dispositions of body and mind that appear requisite for the acquisition of wisdom, yet he recognised, as he goes on to say in verse 21,

[1] Aristotle, edit. E. Bekker I (Berolini 1831) *De Partibus Animalium* 691*b*15
[2] Aristotle, *ibid.*, *Historia Animalium* 608*a*27

that these are insufficient of themselves, and that it is only by the gift of God that it can be obtained.

But before making this further statement he has put in an intermediate sentence, 'Nay rather, being good, I came into a body undefiled'. This contains a more accurate enunciation of what had been already said in the preceding sentence. It is not a correction annulling the previous statement. If the author had thought that what he had written was false or definitely incorrect, he would not have left it but would have simply erased it and written a new sentence that expressed his true mind. Therefore the new sentence is added only to eliminate the possibility of misunderstanding what he had already written. An example of μᾶλλον δὲ introducing a new clause which leaves the first unannulled is seen in Eph 4:28 : 'Let him that stole steal no more : but rather let him labour working with his hands'.

So the question arises what did the author see in his first sentence that might be misunderstood ? In the first place, the word ἔλαχον might be misunderstood. The original meaning was 'to obtain by lot' ; hence the RV 'a good soul fell to my lot'. But the word came to be used simply in the sense of 'to become possessed of' without any idea of chance. And as the writer knew that God's Providence rules all events, this latter is the meaning he intended. Still, the word is in itself ambiguous. In the second place, the grammatical subject of the two verbs would also give ground for second thoughts. In the words, 'I was a well-grown youth' the subject is the whole person made up of body and soul for the youth was a living human being. Then in the following sentence 'and I obtained a good soul' the subject logically excludes the soul, for the soul cannot be said to obtain itself. Thus if pressed, the subject would seem to be the body. This again might be taken to imply that the writer gives the pre-eminence to the body over the soul as if a well-formed body had a previous claim on a correspondingly well-endowed soul. But this would be quite against the writer's mind. He knew that the essential part of man is his soul and that after the separation of body and soul it is the souls of the just which are in the hand of God while their bodies remain in the grave, 3:1. So he rewrites his sentence : 'Nay rather, being good, I came into a body undefiled'. As when the souls of the just are in the hands of God it is their persons who enjoy this privilege, although separated from their bodies, so also in considering the formation of man in the womb it is more accurate to speak of the soul as the person than the body. It is the good soul that according to the harmony of creation is fitted to receive a good body rather than the other way round.

Note that there is question only of good natural endowments, not of moral virtue acquired by practice, as some authors have thought. The introduction of virtue here upsets the writer's argument, for the acquisition and possession of virtue is an essential part of wisdom, and this the speaker has not yet attained, as he makes plain in verse 21. His natural endowments do not suffice ; he must beg wisdom of God. Thus the words cannot mean that the speaker acquired a good virtuous soul by the struggle against evil inclinations and by acquired mastery over them. Nor can they mean that the virtuous soul acquired such control over the body that it succeeded in making of it a body undefiled.

The sense outlined above suits the context, as already indicated, and introduces no idea alien to it. Although the speaker (Solomon) had every natural advantage for the acquisition of wisdom, he recognised their insufficiency as he knew that wisdom may be had only as a gift of God and therefore must be sought from Him in prayer. On the contrary, the opinion that the author here introduces the teaching of the pre-existence of souls supposes him to have digressed from his theme to insist on a belief which has no connection with it. Further, had he intended to introduce this doctrine, he would surely have worded it more clearly. 'I came into a body undefiled'. These very same words could have been written by one who believed that the soul was created after the body, for instance when the human frame had already attained some development in the womb. This was the teaching of Aristotle : 'The body comes into existence before the soul'.[1] This reason alone

[1] *τὸ σῶμα πρότερον τῇ γενέσει τῆς ψυχῆς*, *Politica* VII 15 (edit. I Bekker II 1334*b*20f.)

suffices to show that, widely held though it has been, the belief in the presence here of the doctrine of pre-existence is wide of the mark. None the less it will be as well to add the further consideration that the general doctrine of the Book of Wisdom is quite different from that of Plato and Philo, a fact which makes it more than unlikely that he followed them in the acceptance of the belief in the pre-existence of souls against the teaching of the Bible and the main stream of Jewish tradition. According to Plato and Philo only souls with base tendencies descend to earth to be conjoined with bodies; according to the Book of Wisdom the soul was good at its union with the body. According to the former, souls were by nature destined for an independent existence; according to the latter the union of body and soul appears as the inevitable course of nature. Hence whereas for the philosophers the union is a degradation and defilement of the soul, in the teaching of our author a good soul is happily conjoined with a body undefiled. Again, in the opinion of those who find the pre-existence of souls taught in 8:20 the 'I' is the soul ('I came into a body undefiled'), for, if the body is the prison and tomb of the soul, it is no proper part of the person. But in 7:2 we read 'in the womb of a mother was I moulded into flesh' (RV).[1] It could not be said of the pre-existing soul that it was moulded into flesh.

The conclusion is that for these various reasons it cannot have been the intention of the author to introduce into 8:20 the idea of the pre-existence of souls.[2]

[1] In Swete's edition 7:1: ἐγλύφην σάρξ. That is quite literally 'I was moulded flesh'.

[2] The editor (Holmes) of the book in R. H. Charles (edit.) *Apocrypha and Pseudepigrapha of the Old Testament* I (Oxford 1913) 531 says of 8:19–20: 'These words seem decisive' in showing the writer's belief in the pre-existence of the soul. (His actual words are 'it assumes the existence of the soul before birth', but his meaning is 'before the formation of the body'). His bibliography may be seen, pp. 533f. The contrary view is maintained by the two following writers, P. Heinisch, *Die griechische Philosophie im Buche der Weisheit* (Münster i, W. 1908; Alttestamentliche Abhandlungen I 4) 83–99. Various views given in this study are abandoned in the same writer's later volume, *Das Buch der Weisheit übersetzt und erklärt* (Münster i. W. 1912; Exegetisches Handbuch zum Alten Testament) 170–7. R. Cornely, S.J., *Comm. in Librum Sapientiae*, edit. F. Zorell, S.J. (Parisiis 1910; Cursus Scripturae Sacrae) 326–32. Both writers enumerate supporters of the two opposed views.

Chapter XI

RECAPITULATION

The reader who has followed the theme so far may be glad of a summary of the preceding chapters. Sufferings, afflictions, tribulations are a part of man's daily experience, and it is only to be expected therefore that occasion should often recur in the Bible to speak of them. And such is actually the case. We learn of their origin, their meaning, the spirit in which they should be faced and borne, the reward that awaits endurance with due Christian resignation.

As God created man, suffering had no part in his life. After victory over some temptation or temptations by which his fidelity to his Creator would have been tested and proved, and after a happy life here of unknown duration he would have passed from this world to a better and more felicitous existence with God. But in spite of all his advantages and in spite of the manifest folly of disobedience to the just command of his Benefactor man yielded to the first suggestion of evil. In punishment of this rebellion he lost the privileges of integrity, immortality, and their accompanying advantages, and so was ushered in the condition of this world as we know it. For by the solidarity of the human race our first parents lost their state of terrestrial blessedness not only for themselves but for their posterity also. It was not possible for the two states to exist together, that of primeval felicity and that of fallen humanity. Through the malice of the devil and the weakness and ingratitude of man death and suffering thus came to hold sway in the world.

The effects of corporate solidarity were not confined to the first sin. Throughout history and into our own times it has continued and must continue to be a potent influence in human affairs. Hence it happens that suffering justly merited by the sins of some may and does involve others. In such cases what is a just punishment for some, for it was as punishment that suffering first came into the world, is for others, involved with them, not a punishment but a trial. The actual suffering may be the same for the two classes, but its purpose is quite different. For the one class it is a penalty inflicted in vindication of the moral order ; for the other it is no mark of divine displeasure but an inevitable result of membership of some human group. For them it is a trial of virtue which duly faced and borne issues in new spiritual strength and a grandeur of moral worth that might never have been attained without such testing. An instance of this distinction is clear in the case of the execution of a criminal and a martyr. The mode of execution and the accompanying suffering may be the same in both cases. Yet for the one the infliction of death is a degradation, for the other it is the occasion of undying glory.

In the case of Israel the sense of national, tribal, and family solidarity was strong. And God promised the people as a whole rewards for obedience to His law and faithful observance of the covenant entered into by Him with the nation, and on the other hand threatened the nation as a whole with punishments should they flout their obligations. And men expected the members of a family to share in the lot owing to the merits or demerits of its head. But individual responsibility was known and appreciated from the beginning with corresponding individual punishment or reward. Thus Noe was saved out of the midst of a wicked generation and Lot escaped the destruction that fell on the sinful cities of the plain. Various crimes were to be punished by the death of the offender alone according to the covenant legislation set forth in the Book of Exodus. In the time of Jeremias and Ezechiel, however, individual responsibility was insisted on with new emphasis. The need for this special insistence sprang from the conditions of the time. The troubles and calamities which the sins of the nation had brought on it, led men wrongly to excuse themselves as if they were suffering not for their own wrongdoing but for the sins of their fathers. And this new stressing of each man's responsibility was not intended to do away with all sense of corporate responsibility. It still remained possible that a given generation might suffer not more than it deserved but more than it might have suffered owing to the mercy and long-suffering of God, had not the continued and growing sinfulness of the nation filled its cup of iniquity to the full and at last called down on it the just sentence of God.

Suffering was thus recognised to be the just chastisement of sin and national calamity to be the just result of national infidelity, though this, given the working of the law of solidarity, involved the suffering of innocent members of the nation as well. But it was long before men came to an understanding of the unmerited afflictions of persons who suffered without being involved in any national calamity. As suffering is inflicted in punishment of sin, there was tendency among the people to regard all suffering in the same light. This, of course, was unjustified, as the fact that some suffering is punishment does not warrant the deduction that all suffering is so also. This mentality is reflected in some of the psalms which promise prosperity and happiness to the righteous. The doctrine is fundamentally true and sound, but at the time could not be given its full development for the reason that as yet there had been no revelation concerning rewards and punishments after death. Owing to the incompleteness of the doctrine, as other psalms make manifest, the inequalities of experience provided a problem to religious speculation and even a trial for the faith of some. The nobler souls clung to their certain knowledge that God is good and just and that, even though the reasons for His disposition of events may not be clear to our feeble understanding, His ways are indubitably right and will be justified in the eyes of all in His own good time. Wicked men, however, took advantage of their own prosperity to harden themselves in their wickedness, persuading themselves that they had nothing to fear from the divine justice. God created the world, so they argued, but was too transcendent, too elevated in His celestial abode, to occupy Himself with the affairs of men. This is what was meant by the statement that there is no God, no divine power, that is, active in the government of the world.

One answer to these early deists was provided for those with eyes to see and hearts to understand by the sufferings of such a man as Jeremias. He had been deputed by God for a special mission, to save his people from their sins and from destruction. He had given himself whole-heartedly to the cause even to the sacrifice of a home and wife of his own. His conduct was completely unselfish and beyond the reproach even of the carping. Yet his life was full of trouble, of persecution, of suffering. No one could imagine that his own sins were at the root of his afflictions. His sufferings were in the course of his labours for his people. Yet though not in punishment for personal sins of his own, neither were his sufferings for the sins of the people in the sense of being vicariously undergone for them. Of this there is no trace in his history. It was clear, then, that suffering was not necessarily a sign of God's displeasure and that in no sense was it an indication that God could not or at least did not interest himself in the welfare of His creatures or was not the guardian of the moral order. But there remained a problem, as Jeremias himself felt.

Clear progress towards an ultimate solution is found in prophecies of the Book of Isaias concerning the mission and sufferings of the Servant of the Lord. His mission is to be not only to his own nation but to take the light to, to be the light of, the Gentiles. His task, like that of Jeremias, will be opposed and his efforts met with reproaches and opposition. In spite of all he will persevere setting his face boldly towards the accomplishment of the work committed to him. But neither will his enemies relax their opposition until at last they bring him to a shameful death. But this time it is made plain what the purpose of the suffering and death is. It is not for sins of the sufferer himself, for he is innocent. He bears the iniquity of us all. By his stripes we are healed. His suffering is vicarious.

The question arises naturally here, what is the value of such suffering? How does it attain its end? It is certainly not that God desires His creatures to suffer. It was His intention that they should not suffer at all. But suffering is the natural atonement for sin. Sin means the seeking and exercise of our own will in opposition to the divinely established norm of right and wrong. To redress the balance it is fitting that the sinner should submit to what is against his own will and desire, and suffering is pre-eminently against man's natural inclination and will. But how can atonement be made by one person for sins which are not his own? We must answer that it depends entirely on the good pleasure of God. There is no intrinsic necessity demanding the acceptance of vicarious atonement. In the case of our Blessed Lord the merit of the atonement He offered was of infinite value, being the voluntary act of God made man. In the second place, being the offering of the Second Adam, the Head of the human race in the supernatural order as Adam was in the natural, it could be accepted as atonement for the whole human race not merely on account of its infinite intrinsic worth more than sufficing as atonement for all human evil but also in virtue of Christ being the representative of all mankind and summing up the race in His own Person. And, in the third place, being the act of the Son of God in human form such voluntary self-oblation could not but be most acceptable to God the Father. But, of course, this atonement does not work in any mechanical way. Man cannot persist in sin and flatter himself that his iniquity has been atoned for by the all-precious Passion and Death of Christ. The merits of Christ's sufferings have to be applied to our individual souls and have to be willingly embraced by us, which means that we have to put away the life of sin and live a life of holiness in conformity with God's holy law.

To return now to our summary, we have seen that Suffering may be endured in the cause of a great mission and without any relation to faults of him to whom the mission is entrusted. Or again, it may be vicarious suffering endured for others incapable of duly atoning in full for their own sins. Or it may be, as we learn in the Book of Job, a severe testing of virtue. Virtue in prosperity with every need satisfied may seem easy, though in fact life in wealthy circumstances has dangers and temptations of its own. But at least the wealthy man is open to the charge that he practises virtue not for its own sake, not because he knows it to be right, but because he is persuaded that God rewards his rightdoing and that deviation from the path of virtue might cost him his prosperity. So it was in the case of Job, well endowed, as he was, with the good things of this world. But he stood the test. Deprived of all, even of bodily health, he remained true to God and refused to throw off his allegiance, puzzled and anguished though he was, at the apparent lack of justice in God's treatment of him. Another lesson, also stressed in the book, is the medicinal value of suffering. Where there has been fault, it gives the sinner occasion to enter into himself, to reflect on his evil ways, to recognise their folly and so to come to a better frame of mind.

Then late in the pre-Christian period came the new belief in retribution after death with its impact on the problem of the prosperity of the wicked and the afflictions of the just. This doctrine that the just would be welcomed by God after this life and rewarded by Him in a state of felicity whereas the impious would meet with condign punishment altered man's attitude to terrestrial wellbeing. Religion, from being this-worldly, became other-worldly. The prosperity of this life was seen to be but a passing phase of small moment compared to the eternal welfare of the soul in the life to come. Hence, as we see in the Book of Wisdom and in the story of the Maccabean Martyrs, a great change came over the old concepts. An early death was no longer considered a calamity. Oppression of the just by the wicked lost much of its sting. The just were no longer thought to die but to pass from one life to a better. Only the really wicked should be said to die, for they pass by the loss of this life to a perpetual death. And the Martyrs even rejoiced and counted it a privilege to give up this life rather than be untrue to God and His holy laws.

Such was the elevation of doctrine reached at the close of the Old Testament period. It would, of course, be over-optimistic to imagine that these high ideals had penetrated all sections of the population. Indeed, both the writings of the New Testament and of Josephus show that the important Sadducean party, though its following was small, rejected the doctrines of immortality and future retribution. The Pharisees, on the other hand, embraced these doctrines and their authority was acknowledged by the bulk of the population. The other-worldly approach to life, which had already manifested itself in the Old Testament, receives new emphasis in the teaching of the New. The dangers of riches are stressed and the spiritual advantages of poverty inculcated. Such teaching is itself an invitation to a harder life, as poverty and comfort are not bed-fellows. Poverty connotes hardships and trials of various kinds. Christ attempted to prepare the minds of His disciples for a deeper appreciation of the moral value of suffering by the repeated prediction of His own Passion and Death. But these lessons, though remembered, did not sink in at the time they were given, as their thoughts were obsessed by the idea of a totally different outcome of their Master's mission. After His Death our Lord's words about its being for the redemption of many and His Blood being shed for the remission of sins came back to their minds and this time with full appreciation of their meaning. And it may well be that Christ Himself gave them an explanation when He opened to them the meaning of the Scriptures concerning Himself. The lesson was well learnt and the doctrine is writ large across the pages of the New Testament.

Now the fact that the Head of the Mystical Body underwent great suffering carries with it an implication for the members of that Body. The members must needs share in the fortunes of the Head, for Head and members are one, united in the unity of the one Body. Hence the members must have their share of sufferings too ; and Christ foretold that so it must be. But He also promised a great reward and devoted one of the Beatitudes to those who suffer persecution for justice' sake. This mystery of the union of all true Christians with Christ has the further consoling implication that, if the members must suffer with the Head, so also the Head suffers with the members. If the members of His Church are persecuted, Christ Himself is persecuted ; and for this we have His own authority in His question to Paul, 'Why persecutest thou me ?'. We have, then, this great consolation that we do not suffer alone ; our sufferings are not overlooked or forgotten, for He has identified Himself with us, and our sufferings are His sufferings. This, of course, provided our sufferings are for justice' sake and are not the result of our own sin and folly. Thus it is that He was even able to leave to us to make up something of what was lacking to His own personal sufferings. Although His own Passion and Death more than sufficed for the atonement of sin and the redemption of the world, nevertheless He has given to Christians the privilege of helping by their sufferings, which He reckons as His own, in the application of the fruits of His redemption for the salvation of mankind.

Other motives too are put before us Christians to encourage us in faithful endurance. As in the Old, so also in the New Testament virtue is tested, purified, and strenghtened in the fire of tribulation and affliction. Christ Himself did not disdain to learn obedience by suffering. The remembrance of the reward to come should also help us to constancy and perseverance, for 'our present light tribulation worketh for us above measure exceedingly an eternal weight of glory'.

Not only are we invited to bear with patience and even joy the sufferings that come upon us, but we are further invited to strengthen our spiritual fibre by voluntary self-denial, by willing effort to obtain mastery over our lower nature through the refusal to yield to our desires and cravings even in things quite legitimate. Among other means recommended is fasting, which was already in honour among the Jews. The acceptance of virginity for the sake of the Gospel is highly extolled and temporary abstinence is commended to married folk that they may more readily give themselves to prayer. Our Lord's praise of poverty was taken to heart so earnestly by the early Christians that at Jerusalem all who had lands or houses sold them and laid the price thereof at the feet of the Apostles for the common good. These and all forms of Christian asceticism are combined in Christ's all-embracing invitation to self-abnegation 'If any man will come after me, let him deny himself and take up his cross and follow me'. To penetrate to the full significance of this saying we have to bear in mind that the same word, also with the predicate as direct object, is used of Peter's denial of his Master. In that denial he declared that he had no knowledge of Him, he repudiated Him. Such in brief is the attitude to self which Christ proposes to His disciples.

To complete this short survey it must be added that in the New Testament as in the Old suffering is sometimes the punishment of sin. On the other hand, we are quite clearly warned not to fall into the error of arguing from affliction to sin and supposing that every unfortunate person is paying the penalty of some misdemeanour.

Finally, a fitting close to the New Testament teaching on our subject is provided by St John's vision of the heavenly glory of those who are come out of great tribulation and have washed their robes and have made them white in the Blood of the Lamb.

INDEX

(A separate Scripture index is on page 174)

Index

SCRIPTURE INDEX

Scripture Index

Printed in Great Britain by
Thomas Nelson and Sons Ltd, Edinburgh